2010

"The Suicidal
Plant"
by
Mayer Hillman
Tina Fawcett
Sudhir Chella Rajan

Large Print

Social
Action

2010

THE SUICIDAL PLANET

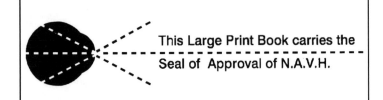

THE SUICIDAL PLANET

HOW TO PREVENT GLOBAL CLIMATE CATASTROPHE

MAYER HILLMAN
WITH TINA FAWCETT
AND SUDHIR CHELLA RAJAN

THORNDIKE PRESS
An imprint of Thomson Gale, a part of The Thomson Corporation

Detroit • New York • San Francisco • New Haven, Conn. • Waterville, Maine • London

LIBRARY OF CONGRESS CATALOGING-IN-PUBLICATION DATA

Hillman, Mayer.
 The suicidal planet : how to prevent global climate catastrophe / by Mayer Hillman with Tina Fawcett and Sudhir Chella Rajan. — Large print ed.
   p. cm.
 Includes bibliographical references and index.
 ISBN-13: 978-0-7862-9670-5 (hardcover : alk. paper)
 ISBN-10: 0-7862-9670-4 (hardcover : alk. paper)
 1. Global warming — Prevention. 2. Global warming — Government policy. I. Fawcett, Tina. II. Rajan, Sudhir Chella, 1961– III. Title.
 QC981.8.G56H55b 2007
 363.738'74—dc22   2007014862

Published in 2007 by arrangement with St. Martin's Press, LLC.

Printed in the United States of America on permanent paper
10 9 8 7 6 5 4 3 2 1

CONTENTS

ACKNOWLEDGMENTS

The authors wish to pay special tribute to Aubrey Meyer, the founder and director of the Global Commons Institute, for the inspiration of his ideas, his contribution to chapters 6 and 7, and the constructive discussions held with him since 1990.

We also wish to record our warm appreciation for the background research work undertaken by Deepak Rughani (environmental consultant) and Catherine Bottrill (researcher at the Environmental Change Institute, University of Oxford) during the preparation of the manuscript for this book; for the very helpful advice given by Sivan Kartha (Tellus Institute, Boston); and especially for invaluable editorial help from Josh Hillman.

Policy Studies Institute in London, the Environmental Change Institute at the University of Oxford, and the Tellus Institute in Boston provided the research bases for the authors.

INTRODUCTION

Climate change is the most important issue of our age, perhaps of any age. If we — individually and collectively — do not act resolutely, extensively, and urgently, the prospects are grim. Average worldwide temperatures could be 10°F above current levels by the end of the century. But even if half of this increase is reached, which is now becoming increasingly probable, this will set in motion a series of devastating effects. Sea levels will rise inexorably and rainfall patterns will be destabilized, with drought conditions and severe flooding far more common. Certain parts of the globe are likely to become uninhabitable, particularly densely populated delta and other low-lying regions. As the planet has only a finite capacity to absorb greenhouse gas emissions without destabilizing the climate, there is the very real prospect that, in the not-too-distant future, the whole world will be faced with catastrophic changes that are irreversible and beyond control.

This is not future-gazing. We are already witnessing the first stages of a disaster of monumental proportions. The greenhouse gases we have been emitting — mainly carbon dioxide from our energy use — will remain in the atmosphere for centuries, in turn causing changes for millennia as the earth slowly reacts. Future generations will bear the heaviest burden for the present generation's irresponsibility. Time is of the essence. Every year that goes by without an appropriate response reduces the chances of averting an ecological Armageddon and makes the changes required by current and future inhabitants of the planet an increasingly uphill struggle.

None of this is the view of alarmists. It is the considered opinion of international climate scientists, now acknowledged by most governments around the world. Nor is it new. In 1993, Al Gore, then American vice president, observed that our civilization is in denial about its addiction to the consumption of the planet's nonrenewable resources bringing us to the brink of catastrophe. In emphasizing the need for the development of a strategic environmental initiative, he wrote: "Only the radical rethinking of our relationship with nature can save the earth's ecology for future generations."

Since then, global warming and its implications have risen up the political and public agendas. There is now no shortage of rhetoric — whether from politicians, the media, or business leaders — about the importance of the environment. But, remarkably, an air of procrastination still prevails. Greenhouse gas emissions are accumulating at a startling rate, but, in the absence of radical policy change, our day-to-day lives continue as usual. The apparent contradiction between awareness and action can only be explained either by a hope that climate change will turn out to be an ephemeral problem that will somehow disappear, or by a belief that extreme climate change can be prevented as the economy grows because technological advances will enable us to continue enjoying our ever-rising standards of living.

These two myths represent wishful thinking and we challenge both. There is plenty of evidence that climate change is already occurring and its impacts will accelerate in the coming decades. Meanwhile, any objective appraisal of the prospective scope of technology reveals that its contribution to the requisite cuts in carbon emissions in the relevant timescale is limited. This is not to discount its value but to stress the far greater need for us to lower our demand for fossil fuels radically. This will require a fundamental reevaluation of the character and quality of our way of life.

We have written this book because the implications of climate change due to human activity are not taken seriously enough. It is a matter of necessity that greenhouse gases are reduced sufficiently to protect the planet from the devastating consequences of climate change. We also consider it a moral issue: It is our responsibility to see it as such. The difficult issues, where a more complex mix of moral, political, and scientific questions arises, are deciding by how much, by when, and by whom. For a start, should it be the most "energy profligate" nations and individuals who should be obliged to bear the greater burden in the reduction of emissions?

Meanwhile, we need to face up to the fact that the radical transition to far less energy-intensive lifestyles will not happen on a voluntary basis as a result of the aggregate decisions of the billions of people living on the planet today. It will take a major policy commitment from governments around the world to ensure that the requisite changes in the behavior of all citizens are made, particularly about how much energy is used in travel and in keeping warm in the winter and cool in the summer. Individuals will need to call for, accept, and, indeed, welcome rigorous government intervention to achieve sufficient carbon dioxide savings across society with everyone making their fair contribution to the savings. We cannot ignore this issue of fair distribution, both internationally and between generations, of a commodity to which, without question, everyone has an equal claim.

Clearly, climate change is a global problem, the solution to which requires agreement by all countries. We present a radical and innovative strategy that we believe is the only one with a realistic prospect of success. Its framework, called *Contraction and Convergence,* consists of a year-on-year "contraction" of carbon dioxide emissions by a chosen date, ratcheting down to relatively safe levels, and targeted at the same time as "convergence" is progressively delivered according to a system of personal carbon allowances of the emissions. It is both a transparent and fair international way of reducing greenhouse gas emissions. It is already commanding wide public support around the world. We believe that negotiations on its adoption cannot be deferred much longer.

Some of the messages in this book might at first seem unwelcome, for we challenge the deep complacency in society that we can continue with energy-profligate lifestyles and "get away with it." However, the book is essentially optimistic. We believe that, with a proper appreciation of the real options open to us, individuals in both developed and developing countries will fully understand and accept the rationale behind the strategy proposed and welcome its implementation. At a practical level, the book also provides the tools for individuals to immediately calculate the contribution their own emissions are making to the problem. And, in light of this, we hope that use will be made of the information and advice offered on how to make the cuts that are highly likely to be necessary.

We do of course acknowledge that climate change is not the only problem the planet faces. There are deeply troubling and unrelenting concerns faced by vast sections of humanity, including war, hunger, disease, and genocide. This book will not speak to them directly, although each of these is a potentially indirect longer-term outcome of global warming. But climate change is also distinctive for several reasons. Humanity as a whole has never before faced such a compelling and urgent threat to its very existence. People and ecosystems everywhere will be affected by climate change, albeit to different degrees.

Climate change raises a profound philosophical question about what kind of moral beings we are. On the one hand, we could leave behind for our children and grandchildren a world that is rendered virtually uninhabitable for most and a correspondingly bleak set of social institutions. A small minority of powerful and wealthy individuals will probably try to secure higher ground and resources and build walls around themselves, putting the poor and weak in greater misery than ever before. On the other hand, we could make a unique commitment to saving our planet by making an ethical choice to share our resources equitably. In doing so, we could create a new global order that is based on principles of social justice and humanity, thus paving the way to take serious steps to address other major planetary problems. Indeed, we have an opportunity to save the planet in more ways than one by taking a sensible and ethical approach to climate change.

The book has three parts. "The Problem" sets out evidence of the damaging impacts of climate change and the prospects of these worsening; excessive energy use as the source; and the inadequacy of the public response to the situation, reflecting a disturbing failure of the government to communicate both its gravity and the contribution we individually are making to it. Part II, "Current Strategies," analyzes the role and prospect of technology allowing for the maintenance of our current lifestyles; the extent of the U.S. government's response to the impending crisis; and the international efforts that have been made to avert it. Part III, "The Solution," presents what its authors see as the only strategy that can now address the global problem comprehensively, and sets out the means whereby it can be adopted and brought into force through a system of personal carbon rationing. It highlights why economies around the world need to be fundamentally restructured in a way that differentiates between those elements of growth that are deleterious and those that are beneficial to the future health of the planet. It concludes by questioning the morality of continuing our current lifestyles when doing so can lead only to the planet's being passed on to future generations in a parlous state.

By the time you have finished reading this book, the following twelve key points will have been covered:

1. Why the threat posed by climate change to human welfare and the environment, both in the United States and worldwide, is so grave and immediate.
2. How our use of fossil fuel energy is the main source of the threat.
3. What we use energy for, and the forces that are driving its consumption ever higher.
4. What excuses people use to avoid taking climate change seriously and why these lack validity.
5. Why our current collective response to the threat of climate change and its implications is totally inadequate.
6. Why the technological options for reducing carbon dioxide emissions, such as greater energy efficiency and far more use of renewable energy, are limited in scope.
7. Why only the principle of equity can realistically be applied in international negotiations on reducing

greenhouse gas emissions.

8. How a system of personal carbon allowances based on this principle, and carbon caps for business and the public sector, will ensure that each country contributes its fair share in an international agreement.
9. Who the winners and losers will be under this system.
10. What we can do as individuals to audit our emissions and reduce them.
11. How a transition toward the necessary year-on-year targets aimed at stabilizing the world's climate can be achieved within the limited timescale now remaining.
12. Why complacency and procrastination on the issue of climate change must stop.

We hope you will agree with the case set out in this book and will be encouraged to join in promoting a radical reappraisal of personal, collective, and political decisions from a climate change perspective. Individuals need not only to adapt their lifestyles but, more important, to press for the national and international change that is the only way out of the impasse into which our head-burying instincts have led us. Widespread public support is vital now. Time is running out *fast!*

A Note on Measurement

In all chapters of this book but one, carbon dioxide emissions are measured in metric tons of carbon, that is, tC, following the convention of most published government statistics. The exception is chapter 9, where the emissions are measured in metric tons or kilograms of carbon dioxide, that is, tCO_2 or $kgCO_2$. This is to follow the convention on existing Web sites and books where figures to help individuals calculate their carbon emissions are reported in tCO_2. One metric ton of carbon is equal to 3.67 tCO_2. When reading about carbon dioxide emissions, it is always important to be certain which unit is being used.

A Note on Information Sources

Many of the facts and figures quoted in this book come from publications by government and national and international organizations. A list of sources can be found in the chapter-by-chapter reference list at the end of the book, starting on page 383.

For a list of abbreviations, see the Appendix, pages 379–382.

■ ■ ■ ■

PART I:
THE PROBLEM

■ ■ ■ ■

1

Beyond the Planet's Limits

CLIMATE CHANGE: WHY, HOW, AND WHAT NEXT?

Climate change is the most serious environmental threat that the world has ever faced. The dangers can hardly be exaggerated. Climate scientists predict that by the end of this century, temperatures could rise 10°F worldwide. But even if they rise by "just" 5°F, major parts of the earth's surface could become uninhabitable and many species on the planet could be wiped out. Just within the next fifty years, there will be more heat waves, higher summer temperatures, fewer cold winters, and rising sea levels. As a consequence, hundreds of millions of people will be at serious risk from flooding, there will be a huge loss of life from excessively hot weather, diseases from warmer regions will become established, some species and habitats will be lost forever, and patterns of agriculture and business will have to change radically. And then, before too long, the whole world may face the even greater

dangers of long-term and irreversible catastrophic changes as warming threatens the
Greenland ice shelf, the Gulf Stream, and
the West Antarctic ice sheet.

WHY IS THE CLIMATE CHANGING?

The climate is changing because the natural
mechanism known as the "greenhouse effect" — which warms the earth — is being
increased by human-induced emissions of
carbon dioxide and other gases. As the
concentrations of the emissions rise well
above their natural levels, additional warming is taking place, as shown in the diagram
below.

To explain this effect in somewhat more
detail, the temperature of the earth is
determined by the balance between incom-
ing energy from sunlight and energy constantly being lost from the earth into space.
The energy from the sun can pass through
the atmosphere almost unchanged and
warm the planet. But the heat emanating
from the earth's surface is partly absorbed
by certain gases in the atmosphere and
some of this is returned to earth. This
infrared radiation further warms the planet's
surface and the lower strata of the atmosphere. Without this natural greenhouse effect, the planet would be over 35°F cooler

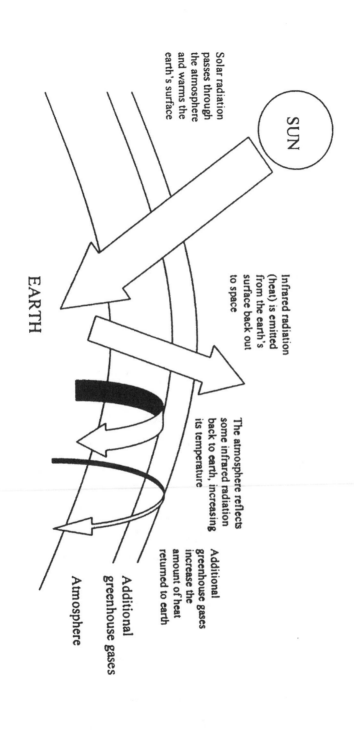

SUN

Solar radiation passes through the atmosphere and warms the earth's surface

EARTH

Infrared radiation (heat) is emitted from the earth's surface back out to space

The atmosphere reflects some infrared radiation back to earth, increasing its temperature

Additional greenhouse gases increase the amount of heat returned to earth

Additional greenhouse gases

Atmosphere

than it is now — too cold for us to inhabit. However, the greenhouse gases we add to the atmosphere mean that more heat is being trapped. This is leading to global warming and other changes to the climate.

The primary cause of these climate changes is our use of coal, oil, and natural gas. Burning these carbon-based fossil fuels results in the production of carbon dioxide. Globally, these emissions contribute more than two-thirds of the warming and, within the United States, they account for five-sixths. Due to their chemical structure, different types of fuel give rise to different amounts of carbon dioxide per ton burned and per unit of energy produced. Coal is the fossil fuel that produces the most carbon dioxide per unit of energy, followed by oil and gas. (Energy use is explored in detail in the next chapter.)

In addition to fossil fuel combustion, land-use changes contribute to the release of carbon dioxide into the atmosphere. These changes stem from clearing land for logging, ranching, and agriculture, or switching from agricultural to industrial or urban use. Vegetation contains carbon that is released as carbon dioxide when it decays or burns. Normally, lost vegetation would be replaced by regrowth, with little or no extra emissions because the replacement vegetation absorbs carbon dioxide from the atmosphere as it grows. However, over the past several hundred years, deforestation and other land-use changes around the world have contributed to one-fifth of the additional carbon dioxide in the atmosphere attributable to human activity, mostly through cutting down tropical forests.

This book concentrates on carbon dioxide emissions from fossil fuel use because these are the largest global source of greenhouse gases. However, it should be noted that, in addition to carbon dioxide, there are five other important greenhouse gases: methane, nitrous oxide, hydrofluorocarbons, per-fluorocarbons, and sulfur hexafluoride. The most significant of these are the first two. Methane emissions come primarily from agriculture, waste, coal mining, and natural-gas distribution. They can be a major component of greenhouse gas emissions in countries with strong agricultural econo-mies. For example, as a by-product of their digestion, New Zealand's forty-five million sheep and eight million cattle produce about 90 percent of that country's methane emissions, which equates to over 40 percent of the country's total production of greenhouse gases. Nitrous oxide is generated from agriculture, industrial processes, and fuel combustion. The other greenhouse gases are emitted from a small range of industrial processes and products. With the exception of methane, these other gases are much easier to control through technological change than is carbon dioxide.

CARBON DIOXIDE EMISSIONS

Concentrations of carbon dioxide in the atmosphere have been increasing since the Industrial Revolution. In 1750, there were 280 parts per million (ppm) but by 2005 the figure was 380 ppm, a rise of over one-third. As can be seen in figure 1, below, much of this staggering increase — measured at Mauna Loa, Hawaii, the meteorological station with the longest records in the world — has taken place since 1959. From 1997 to 1998, there was an increase of 2.87 ppm, the largest single yearly jump ever recorded.

Data have been obtained from measurements of air that has been trapped in ice over thousands of years. These reveal that today's carbon dioxide concentration has not been exceeded in the past 420,000 years

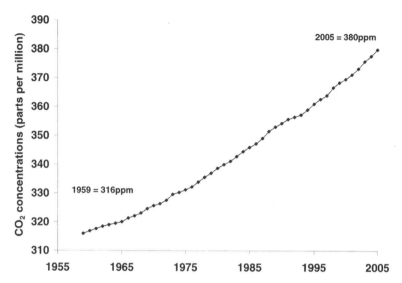

Figure 1: Atmospheric carbon dioxide (CO2) concentrations since 1959, Mauna Loa, Hawaii. Source: Keeling and Whorf, 2005

and probably not during the past 20 million years. As well as the level, the rate of increase over the past century is unprecedented. Compared to the relatively stable carbon dioxide concentrations — in the preceding several thousand years, there were relatively minor fluctuations around the 280 ppm figure — the increase during the industrial era, and particularly the most recent increase, is proving catastrophic.

This phenomenon is perhaps unsurprising. Fossil fuels contain the energy stored from the sun that took hundreds of thousands of years to accumulate, yet within the space of a few generations — a mere blink of the planet's life so far — we are burning it: Figure 2 shows the dramatic and accelerating growth in carbon emissions from fossil fuel use, which is the major source of the accumulating concentrations. Half the total emissions since 1750 have occurred since the mid-1970s, with annual emissions doubling since the mid-1960s and trebling since the mid-1950s. Emissions of carbon dioxide from fossil fuel burning rose from about 10 million tons of carbon a year in 1800 to around 7 billion tons at present, which is 700 times as much. Future scenarios suggest that, unless dramatic policy

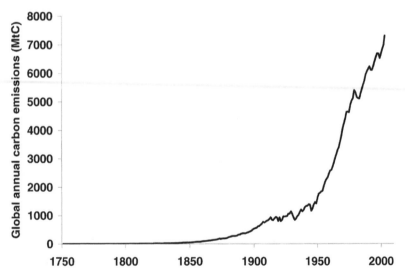

Figure 2: Annual global carbon emissions from fossil fuels (MtC) since 1750. Source: Marland, Boden, and Andres, 2006

changes are made, annual emissions will rise substantially and inexorably. At the extreme, they could be five times their current level by 2100, resulting in the 10°F or so of global warming referred to earlier. In fact, since our atmosphere and oceans take a long time to warm up (and cool down), the effects of these higher emissions could get even worse over time.

At the start of this century, total annual global emissions from fossil fuels amounted to more than 7,000 million metric tons of carbon (MtC). Emissions from North America (United States and Canada) made up over a quarter of the total, and those from Western Europe accounted for about one-tenth. The United States continues to have the highest fossil fuel–related emissions, reaching 1,580 million metric tons of carbon in 2003. This represents nearly a quarter of the world's total. U.S. emissions are two-thirds higher than those of the world's second-largest emitter, the People's Republic of China, and almost seven times those of the whole African continent. In general, emissions from the United States have risen each year since 1900, with the exception of brief periods in the 1930s and 1980s. Since 1990, fossil fuel emissions have risen between 1 and 2 percent each year.

Chapter 2 explains in detail the patterns of changing energy consumption and the underlying trends that have driven this upward and led to the increasing emissions.

Each person in the world is engaged in fossil fuel–based activity that results in the emission of, on average, 1.1 metric tons of carbon. If these emissions are compared by country, the differences are stark. Near the top of the league is the United States, at 5.5 tC per person, around five times the global average. In the fifteen Western European members of the European Union, they are 2.3 tC. The developing nations currently contribute much less, with China's emissions at 0.7 tC per person, Indonesia's at 0.4 tC, and India's at 0.3 tC. Afghanistan is at the bottom of the emissions league, at 0.01 tC, just one one-hundredth of the global average and less than one five-hundredth of that of the average U.S. citizen.

How Is the Climate Changing?
Temperature Changes

Figure 3 shows how the global average surface temperature (over sea and land) has risen from 1850 to the present. Because temperatures vary naturally from year to year, climate scientists must compare several years' temperature records with long-term averages to be sure the suspected temperature change is significant. The data are set out in terms of the "anomaly" — that is, the difference between each year and the average temperature in the period 1961–90. Before 1978, it was generally colder, with all later years warmer. These data are shown in the figure in degrees Celsius, not Fahrenheit: A rise of 0.47°C is equivalent to 0.8°F.

Global temperature, established from millions of individual measurements taken from around the world, rose by about 1.1°F during the last century, with two-thirds of this warming occurring since the 1970s. The 1990s was the warmest decade, with 1998 being the warmest year since 1860, when world temperature measurements were first recorded. Scientists at the University of East Anglia in the United Kingdom, in one of the most comprehensive studies to date of climatic history, have confirmed that the planet is now warmer than it has been at any time in the past 2,000 years. And there is no sign of this trend reversing: nineteen of the twenty hottest years in the past 150 years have occurred since 1980, and 2005 was the warmest year on record in the Northern Hemisphere. Worldwide, temperatures on land have warmed more than the oceans.

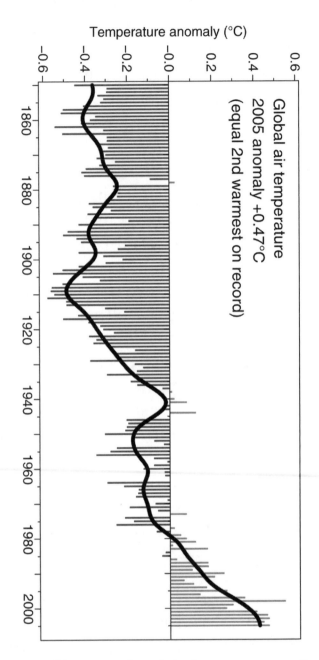

Figure 3: Changes in global average surface air temperature compared with the long-term average for 1961–1990. Source: Climatic Research Unit. See www.cru.uea.ac.uk/cru/info/warming

The United States reflects these trends. Observations from over twelve hundred weather stations across the country have shown that the average temperature rose by almost 1°F during the twentieth century, with annual temperatures in the coastal Northeast, the upper Midwest, the Southwest, and parts of Alaska experiencing increases four times that average. The largest observed warming has been seen in winter.

OTHER CLIMATE CHANGES

Rising temperatures increase the amount of energy in the atmosphere, and this has consequential effects: Climate models predict changes in rainfall amounts and patterns, and a rise in the occurrence of storms, heat waves, and other extreme events. Some of these changes, including periods of sustained drought from higher than average temperatures and well below average rainfall, have already been experienced in the United States and around the world. The most populated state of Australia has recently experienced four years of drought. When persistent droughts occur, there is little reserve water to weather them, leaving people, livestock, and crops at risk. The growing season is then reduced or even lost completely. Because of this, food production in some parts of the developing world is already in decline. The well-known variability of the climate can make it difficult to ascertain that any individual event is unusual and specifically caused by climate change. But the accumulating evidence from studies over the last forty years makes it highly unlikely that the data can be interpreted as the outcome of a natural cycle uninfluenced by human activity.

In the United States, signs of water stress that used to be limited to the West are now increasingly common in the East — from dried-up rivers to shrinking lakes and falling water tables. On the other hand, average precipitation has increased by 5 to 10 percent over the last century, with much of that due to an increase in the frequency and intensity of heavy rainfall. Precipitation increases have been especially noteworthy in the Midwest, southern Great Plains, and parts of the West and Pacific Northwest.

Of particular concern has been the increased frequency and intensity of extreme events, such as storms and hurricanes, as these tend to have severe effects on people and on the man-made environment as well as the natural environment. This concern was intensified as a result of the very active hurricane season and particularly the severe impact of Hurricane Katrina on New Orleans and the surrounding area in 2005. Indeed, 2005 was the most destructive year on record.

Although the number of tropical storms and hurricanes has remained roughly constant in the last thirty years, there has been an increase in their intensity, with a rising proportion having wind speeds above 130 miles per hour. This has been shown to be linked to recorded increases in sea-surface temperatures. Some scientists have established a direct link between climate change and the increasing intensity of hurricanes. Global climate change may also affect other weather systems. El Niño is a complex, natural change in weather patterns that occurs every few years, affecting the equatorial Pacific region and beyond. It caused worldwide damage valued at $32 billion in 1997–98. At present, there is a suspicion, though not yet proof, that El Niño has been made worse by global warming.

SKEPTICS

Climate science, like any other science, is characterized by intense debates that range from the role of clouds and aerosols in calculating the magnitude of the greenhouse effect, to the difficulty of establishing the extent to which observed climatic changes are attributable to human activity. A small but vocal group of lobbyists, called "climate skeptics" by the media, has challenged the consensus on climate change and its causes. Typical of the more influential of these was a senior U.S. government official describing man-made global warming as "the greatest hoax ever perpetrated on the American people." However, groups like the Intergovernmental Panel on Climate Change (IPCC), the American Geophysical Union, the U.S. National Academy of Sciences, and ten other related leading world bodies support two critical scientifically determined judgments: first, that global warming is happening, and second, that much of the observed warming is human induced. They admit that it is difficult to predict some aspects of this human-induced climate change, such as exactly how fast it is occurring, exactly how much it will change, and exactly where the changes will take place.

The skeptics, on the other hand, who have tended in the past to deny both judgments, are now largely in the habit of denying just the second one, on the grounds that climate science itself is too complex for us to be sure that humans are largely responsible for climate change. The Union of Concerned Scientists, a watchdog group of scientists and citizen advocates, has examined a list of the more prominent of these skeptic groups. Its analysis reveals that the great majority either belong to or are actively sponsored or funded by organizations such as the fossil fuel industries, which have a commercial interest in denying the reality of climate change. Though in a very small minority, they are much better known in the press than in scientific journals, suggesting that they have not been able to prove their case using established scientific methods.

Effects of Climate Change on the Natural and Human Environment

Glaciers and Sea Ice

Climate change is now wide-ranging in its impacts. Higher temperatures have already had a measurable effect on land glaciers and sea ice. Mountain glaciers have been shrinking in almost all areas of the world. For example, the glacier from which mountaineers began the first ascent of Everest in 1953 has retreated by about three miles over the past fifty years. There has been a substantial thinning of Arctic sea ice in late summer: In August 2000, for example, there was no ice at the North Pole; there was only a stretch of open water. More generally, sea ice in the Northern Hemisphere has decreased over the last three decades by an area equivalent to that of the state of Texas.

SEA LEVELS

Rising sea levels are due both to the expansion of warmer water in the oceans and to the additional water produced by melting land glaciers. Increasing atmospheric concentrations of greenhouse gases are expected to raise sea levels around the world by a few feet over this century. Studies have shown that as much as a third of the Hawaiian shoreline has already experienced significant loss or narrowing of beaches. On the coast of New Jersey, Delaware, and Maryland, over 80 percent of beaches have experienced erosion over the last 150 years. In other parts of the world, including the South Pacific, the Caribbean, Bangladesh, and vast parts of coastal Africa, sea level rise over the course of this century is expected to be especially devastating, resulting in the creation of millions of "climate exiles."

Global climate change is also disrupting seasonal patterns and the location of fauna and flora. The temperature rise of 1.8°F since 1900 in central England has resulted in spring starting earlier and winter coming later and in plants growing for an extra month each year. Butterflies, birds, and fish are already moving to new habitats to survive. There is also evidence of a decrease in species attuned to northerly conditions: A combination of overfishing and global warming has led to cod stocks in the North Sea falling to one-tenth of what they were thirty years ago. The temperature of the North Sea has risen even more sharply than the air temperature, with the result that cod, a cold-water fish, appear to be migrating northward. At the same time, new fish species from southerly waters have been found in the now-warmer sea off the southwest coast of England.

Changes in behavior have been observed as the climate changes, leading to an increase of some species while others are lost. Arctic pack ice is melting at such a rate that polar bears are starving and could soon become extinct because the animals they feed on, such as seals, are becoming scarce, and there is less ice for the bears to track across to reach them. In the United States, scientists from the University of California at Berkeley found that several species of small mammals have moved to higher altitudes in Yosemite National Park during the last century, possibly owing to climate change. In the same period, a 50 percent turnover in the types of birds harbored in the Sierra Nevada Mountains has been recorded.

DRAMATIC CHANGES IN ALASKA

Temperature changes in Alaska have been among the most dramatic seen anywhere. The climate there has warmed on average by 4°F since the 1950s. Even greater warming, about 7°F, has occurred in the interior in winter. As a consequence, the growing season has lengthened by more than two weeks over the past fifty years. The permafrost that underlies most of this state has thawed extensively, causing increased erosion, landslides, sinking of the ground surface, and damage to forests, buildings, and infrastructure. In some areas, erosion has led to shorelines retreating by more than fifteen hundred feet. Several coastal villages will soon have to be fortified or relocated. Loss of sea ice also has caused large-scale changes in marine ecosystems, threatening populations of mammals that depend on ice and the subsistence livelihoods that depend on them.

Forestry has also been adversely affected. A sustained infestation of spruce bark beetles since 1992 — in the past, limited by lower temperatures — has caused widespread tree deaths across 2.3 million acres on the Kenai Peninsula. This represents the largest loss of insect habitat ever recorded in North America. Significant increases in the frequency and intensity of fires, both related to summer warming, have also occurred. Thus, the rapid warming of Alaska is causing substantial ecological and socioeconomic damage.

What Happens Next?

What will happen next with climate change depends on the following:

- How much more carbon dioxide and other greenhouse gases are released into the atmosphere.
- The developing reaction of global systems to past, present, and future emissions.

We Can't Switch off Climate Change

The effects of climate change cannot quickly be reversed by reducing or even eliminating future emissions of greenhouse gases. There are two reasons for this. First, greenhouse gases released into the atmosphere linger for decades (in the case of relatively short-lived gases like methane), or hundreds of years (for carbon dioxide), or even thousands of years (for the long-lived gases like per-fluorocarbons). Carbon dioxide and methane concentrations in the atmosphere are respectively one-third and more than twice as high as those at any time over the last 650,000 years. Even if no additional carbon dioxide were emitted from now on, atmospheric concentrations would take centuries to decline to pre-Industrial Revolution levels. While elevated levels of greenhouse gases remain in the atmosphere, additional warming will occur.

Second, the planet is slow to adjust to changes in temperature. The delayed effects from the current warming have to reach a state of equilibrium as the extra energy distributes itself between atmosphere, oceans, and land. For this reason, global increases in mean surface temperatures, rising sea levels from thermal expansion of the oceans, and melting ice sheets are projected to continue for hundreds of years. So, even if all fossil fuel use ceased tomorrow, the climate would continue to change. We are changing the climate not just for the next generations but for tens of generations to come with potentially devastating social and economic consequences.

The persistence of greenhouse gases in the atmosphere should determine the action that needs to be taken. Stabilization of carbon dioxide emissions at near-current levels would not lead to the stabilization of atmospheric concentrations. These would go on rising — the "old" carbon dioxide being joined by the "new." Stabilizing concentrations — at any level — requires a reduction of fossil fuel use to a fraction of its current level. Over the next one hundred years or so, emissions need to decline to a safe level, taking into account the uncertain capacity of natural land and ocean sinks to continue to absorb any excess. According to one authoritative estimate, the required reduction is to 200 MtC per annum for the world as a whole — that is about one-eighth of U.S. annual emissions of carbon dioxide!

FUTURE CLIMATE CHANGE AND ITS IMPACTS
The Intergovernmental Panel on Climate Change (IPCC) is an international body of

scientists and other experts that was formed to provide information and advice on climate change. Its reports, referred to in more detail in later chapters, have become the standard works of reference on the subject. It acts as the scientific advisory body for the UN. It suggests that the world's temperature is likely to increase by at least 2.5°F and as much as 10.4°F over the period from 1990 to 2100, depending on which greenhouse gas–emission forecast is closest to the truth. The highest temperature projections would correspond to atmospheric carbon dioxide concentrations of 950 ppm — more than three times pre–Industrial Revolution levels. However, these temperature projections are for the *average* global surface temperature (which includes sea surface); it is very likely that nearly all land areas will warm to a greater extent. This is particularly true in Alaska, Canada, and the northern and central regions of Asia, where land temperatures could rise by 18°F. It is important to put possible temperature changes in perspective: The global temperature difference between the last Ice Age and the present was around 10°F. An increase of 18°F would create conditions in Western Europe comparable to those of the Sahara desert. Half of this increase would be a terrifying prospect. Even more catastrophically, a new climate model developed at the United Kingdom's Hadley Centre for Climate Prediction and Research suggests that this century could see more and faster warming than the IPCC predictions.

The scenarios based on continuing high emissions indicate that many countries will be under threat from rising sea levels, drought, storms, heat waves, and extreme economic and social disruption. Plans are already having to be made for the permanent evacuation and resettlement of the populations of low-lying islands in the Pacific and Indian oceans where no land exists at altitudes that are safe from inundation. Sea levels are predicted to rise by three feet by the end of this century, leading to heavily populated delta areas of the world such as in Bangladesh and China becoming submerged. It has been estimated that 200 million people in these areas could be affected. The problems that this could lead to are obvious.

Humans will not become extinct as a species, but far more of us will die prematurely. A World Health Organization (WHO) report estimated that more than 160,000 people in developing countries are now dying each year from the effects of global warming, including malaria, malnutrition, and extremes of heat and cold. The Earth Policy Institute in Washington, D.C., estimated that 35,000 people died in Europe alone during the record heat wave in the summer of 2003. The WHO predicts that by 2020, the number dying each year around the world from this cause will have almost doubled. Infectious diseases will rise as the world gets warmer and they spread north into higher latitudes.

We are also very likely to run out of comfortable areas of the world in which to live. The outcome of this is a major increase in environmental refugees: One calculation, considered conservative, is that there will be a six-fold increase in current numbers, reaching 150 million by 2050. A huge wave of species extinction could also be set in motion. Researchers at Bristol University in the United Kingdom have shown that 11°F of global warming was enough to wipe out up to 95 percent of all species on the planet at the end of the Permian period, 250 million years ago.

FUTURE IMPACTS ON THE UNITED STATES

The climate in the United States is predicted to be very different toward the end of the century. There is general agreement that more intense storms are likely to be generated as the global climate continues to warm: Events such as Hurricane Katrina can be expected to increase in the future. Further global temperature and sea level rises, combined with ongoing regional post-glacial subsidence, are predicted to continue to erode the coastlines. This inevitably will cause enormous problems for the many cities in highly urbanized coastal areas.

The U.S. National Assessment suggests that U.S. temperatures could increase by 3°F to 9°F. Yet, just 1°F of additional global warming could see drought across the western states that are at present the fastest growing. Deserts will reemerge across the High Plains — in particular Nebraska, which has areas of stabilized sand dunes thousands of years old from paleo-droughts, but also Wyoming, eastern Montana, northern Texas, and much of Oklahoma. (The area covered by desert and subject to intense dust storms in sub-Saharan Africa and Central Asia is already increasing at an alarming rate.) Agriculture would have to be abandoned over millions of square miles of the plains. An increase of 2°F could see major water shortages in California, affecting Los Angeles and San Francisco in particular, and in other states dependent for their freshwater supplies on snowpack runoff from the Sierra Nevada. Snowpack could decline by 70 percent, because winter precipitation would run straight into rivers rather than remain into the summer as snow to keep the rivers running. This would be accompanied by a major increase in heat waves and wildfires. And an increase of 3°F would trigger the destabilization of the Greenland ice sheet, whose eventual melt — over centuries in the conventional view, but possibly much faster — would flood much of Florida and the east coast, including New York and Boston. As a result of more intense hurricanes causing massive storm surges, a massive loss of life and New Orleans–style devastation across much of this heavily populated coast is possible.

In addition, while varying across the United States, both precipitation and evaporation are projected to rise, and occurrences of unusual warmth and extreme wet and dry conditions to become more frequent. Alaska is expected to continue to experience more dramatic changes in climate than most other U.S. states. These are likely to experience changes similar to an overall northern shift in weather systems and climate conditions. For example, the central tier of states would experience climate conditions roughly equivalent to those now experienced in the southern tier. Summertime will become extremely uncomfortable in the southern states due to a combination of increasing temperatures and rising humidity. Predicted consequences include serious damage to agriculture, water resources, human health, wildlife, and the countryside, which will be progressively more expensive to deal with, and outbreaks of malaria and increasing numbers of deaths from heatstroke (though the warmer winters should reduce deaths from cold temperatures).

THE UNINHABITABLE PLANET?

All the forecasts above are based on the climate continuing to respond in a predictable way to increasing temperatures, with no unexpected shocks or "positive feedback" in the climate system (self-reinforcing and accelerating effects). However, current understanding of climate change is not reliable enough to be sure that something unexpected will not take place. In fact, geological records show that fast changes in climate have occurred in the past. Grounds for even greater concern are supported by recent research in related fields.

The Role of Carbon Sinks

At present, about half of our man-made emissions of carbon dioxide remain in the atmosphere, leading to the increasing concentrations shown in figure 1 (see page 29). The remaining carbon dioxide is absorbed by the land and oceans, which act as "carbon sinks." However, there has never been any guarantee that as atmospheric levels of carbon dioxide rise, these sinks will continue to absorb carbon dioxide at the same rate. Like a saturated sponge, they could lose their power of absorption.

The concern is that the capacity of these sinks is already reducing. Some evidence indicates that far fewer emissions from fossil burning appear to be retained. Possible explanations are increased forest combustion and the warming and acidification of oceans. The effect of reducing sinks is that more of each ton of carbon dioxide emitted will stay in the atmosphere. Therefore the effects of greenhouse gas emissions on temperature could be even more extreme than currently expected.

Other Grounds for Concern

Evidence from three recent studies suggests further disturbing scenarios for later this century. First, vast quantities of methane (a greenhouse gas twenty times more potent than carbon dioxide) are stored in sediments below the shallow seabed of the Arctic and below the tundra in northern Canada and Siberia, according to the U.S. Geological Survey. When the temperature surrounding the methane warms, it becomes unstable and methane gas is released, causing temperatures to increase further. A vast expanse of western Siberia is already undergoing an unprecedented thaw. An area of permafrost spanning a million square kilometers — the size of France and Germany combined — has started to melt for the first time. This thawing is allowing the underlying methane to escape, in the process contributing to a real risk of devastation by global warming.

Second, a newly identified phenomenon of "global dimming" reported in early 2005 indicates that the average amount of sunlight reaching the earth between 1960 and 1990 declined by 4 to 6 percent, owing to the atmosphere being polluted by emissions of sulfur dioxide. Some scientists now consider that this has masked the effect of global warming to some extent and that resolving global dimming may therefore lead to increases in predictions of future temperatures. It has been observed that, while most of the earth has warmed, the regions downwind from major sources of air pollution (specifically sulfur dioxide emissions), such as the eastern United States, have warmed less than other areas.

Third, the benefits of the Gulf Stream, which transports warm water from the tropics to northwestern Europe, providing it with relatively mild winters in relation to its latitude, could be reduced or even lost. The most recent evidence shows that the freshwater from the melting ice caps in the Arctic is disrupting this natural process. The Gulf Stream has weakened by 30 percent in the last twelve years — a far faster rate of change than scientists had expected to see. This could lead to a cooling by 9°F within a few decades — a return to the Ice Age, in northwestern Europe.

SAFE LIMITS?

Is there a "safe" limit for carbon dioxide and other greenhouse gas concentrations in the atmosphere? Determining the safe limit depends on the sensitivity of the climate to greenhouse gases and the rate at which some of these gases get sequestered in sinks. According to the 2001 report by the IPCC, a rise of average global temperatures by 2 degrees Celsius (3.6 degrees Fahrenheit) over preindustrial levels is an important threshold, beyond which damage to human health and the planet's ecosystems would be especially dangerous. Scientists have estimated the upper limit for carbon dioxide concentrations that would correspond to a rise of no more than 2 degrees Celsius. Until recently, a figure of 550 ppm was thought to be safe. However, as scientific understanding of climate change advances, the safe-concentration figure has fallen dramatically. Now, 400–450 ppm is thought to be the safe limit. At current rates of increase, we are only about ten years away from global carbon dioxide concentrations of 400 ppm.

As understanding of climate change continues to advance, the safe limit might well reduce further — requiring even faster and deeper cutbacks in carbon dioxide emissions. Of course, the only truly safe limit would be a return to preindustrial levels of emissions, but this is unlikely ever to be achieved. However, in this book we assume that our aim as a world community should be to reduce carbon dioxide emissions sufficiently to ensure that a concentration of 400–450 ppm is not exceeded. Chapter 9 discusses in more detail what this would mean for the United States — but the carbon emissions reductions required from Americans as part of a worldwide agreement would be 80 percent by 2030. This challenging target sets the context for the remainder of this book. Very radical changes to current patterns of fossil fuel use and consequent carbon emissions are required if we are to avoid dangerous levels of climate change.

CONCLUSIONS

A consensus now exists in the scientific community that global warming is occurring — with frightening consequences. The problem stems from man-made activities exaggerating the planet's natural greenhouse characteristics that have so far enabled it to support life. Scientists have established that the planet has only a finite capacity to absorb greenhouse gas emissions without causing catastrophic results not only for the natural world but for humanity itself. This chapter has drawn attention to the weight of evidence on this. It is too overwhelming to justify inaction or to propose a "no regrets" policy of taking only those preventive measures known to be cost-effective. Hurricane Katrina, in 2005, showed that no country can expect to be spared from its adverse impacts.

This chapter's main points are:

- Concentrations of carbon dioxide in the atmosphere are over one-third higher than they were at the start of the Industrial Revolution.
- The increase has been caused by human activities, primarily the burning of fossil fuels. Their use and the global emissions of carbon dioxide that stem from it are rising quickly.
- The enhanced greenhouse effect has already caused an average of 1.1°F of warming around the world.
- Trends in emissions are currently on the worst possible path, risking atmospheric carbon dioxide concentrations of 950 ppm by 2100, with associated average temperature rises of up to 10°F or more.
- If no action is taken to reduce greenhouse gas emissions, this increase could be in excess of the temperature difference between the last Ice Age and now. This would be disastrous for the climate, the environment, and the world's population.
- The impacts of climate change on the human and natural environment are

already striking — ranging from a worldwide retreat of glaciers and a marked increase in extreme weather events to alarming changes in the seasons.

- If there are catastrophic and unexpected changes to the climate system, which cannot be ruled out, the future looks even bleaker.
- In the United States, each person's contribution to carbon dioxide emissions is about five times the world average.

Radical and urgent action is needed to ensure that we do not make much of the planet uninhabitable. Chapter 2 looks at current energy use and its contribution to greenhouse gases in order to see what that scale of change has to be to ensure that future carbon dioxide emissions do not exceed the planet's capacity to absorb them without causing serious disruption of its ecological balance.

2

As If There's No Tomorrow

ENERGY USE: PAST, PRESENT, AND FUTURE

Human beings have an increasingly voracious appetite for energy. We probably used more in the last century — especially in North America and Europe — than in the preceding one hundred centuries combined, the vast majority of it in the last few decades, mostly from burning fossil fuels. It is this increasing dependency that makes drastic curtailment of the use of fossil fuels such a challenge. What follows is an attempt to trace and understand this enormous surge in global energy consumption. As this book is concerned with how we as individuals can make a difference to climate change, this chapter focuses in more detail on the energy used in the home and for transport. The profile of energy usage in the past, present, and future, especially in countries such as the United States, points to a continuation of its upward trend and consequent increases in carbon dioxide emissions.

Our excessive fossil fuel consumption is not the only cause for grave concern. There are other alarming effects with the consumption of land, fish stocks, and freshwater also reaching their limits. There is a measure called the "ecological footprint," which shows the combined impact of consumption of energy and material resources. The application of this measure reveals the extent of our predicament: If everyone on the planet consumed as much as each person in the United States, we would need five planets from which to produce the resources and deal with the waste.

WORLD ENERGY USE

The key measure of world energy use is the demand for "primary energy" — the measure of the total consumed, including what is used or lost in the production process, such as in the generation of electricity for the end user. Demand for commercially traded primary energy has doubled from 5,000 million metric tons of oil equivalent (mtoe) in 1970 to 10,500 mtoe in 2005 (see figure 4, below). Traditional fuels such as firewood, animal dung, and peat are not included in this graph because the data are not available. Oil remains the single largest source of energy, accounting for over one-third of the total, followed by natural gas and coal, which each supply around one-quarter of global energy. Since 1970, natural gas has become relatively more important as a global fuel, and the role of nuclear power and hydroelectricity has also increased.

Most of the increase in consumption during this period is accounted for by the Asia Pacific countries, where it has more than quadrupled, and North America (United States, Canada, and Mexico), where it has increased by around 50 percent. For western European countries, it has increased by 40

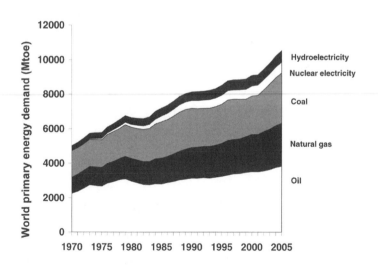

Figure 4: World primary energy consumption, 1970–2005.
Source: BP Statistical review of world energy, 2006

percent, due mainly to rising demand in France, Spain, and Italy. Despite these changes, until 2002, North America remained the region with the highest share of energy consumption (only then overtaken by Asia Pacific), and Africa remained by far the lowest. Regional shares in 2005 were:

North America: 27 percent
Asia Pacific: 33 percent
European Union (25 countries): 16 percent
Africa: 3 percent
Rest of the world: 21 percent

There are massive variations in energy usage per person across countries. The United States is one of the highest: in 2004, the average American used 7.9 metric tons of oil equivalent (toe), the United Kingdon was half that at 3.8, China was much lower at 1.0, with Bangladesh accounting for only 0.11.

WHY ARE WE USING MORE ENERGY?

World energy use is a function of a complex relationship between population, economic growth, and technology. Before the Industrial Revolution, both population and economic growth were relatively slow. But world population has grown apace: Over the last two hundred years it has increased six-fold and now stands at over six billion. However, during this period, economic growth was sufficiently rapid to raise the standards of living of the vast additional numbers of people. This was made possible by new technologies and systems of economic organization associated with the wider availability of energy from fossil fuels. The Industrial Revolution was first powered by coal and, from the late nineteenth century, by oil and natural gas. Economic growth, particularly during the twentieth century, could not have occurred without these newly identified sources of fossil fuel. In other words, their increased usage is a cause as well as a consequence of increasing economic activity.

THE U.S. ENERGY PROFILE

This chapter looks at all forms of energy — fossil fuels, nuclear, and renewables — though the latter two are discussed in more detail in a later chapter. Energy use in the United States from 1970 to 2005 rose by almost 50 percent (see figure 5 below). It can be seen that the contribution of gas has not changed much — growth has come through oil, coal, and nuclear energy.

Oil was the largest source of energy in 1970 and still is. Renewable sources provided 6 percent of energy needs in both 1970 and 2005. Natural gas usage has remained steady, resulting in its percentage contribution to national supplies falling, while coal usage has expanded to provide 23 percent of national primary energy in 2005. Nuclear electricity has increased from a very small contribution in 1970 to 8 percent of primary energy by 2005. The change in the mix of fuels has stemmed largely from the change in the fuels used for

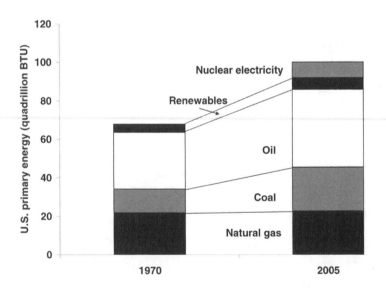

Figure 5: U.S. primary energy demand, 1970 and 2005. **Source: Energy Information Administration of the U.S. Government [EIA], Annual Energy Review, 2005**

electricity generation and for heating. The fuel used for transport remains unchanged as, at present, there are no significant alternatives to gasoline and diesel for motor vehicles and to kerosene for aircraft.

Due to their chemical structures, coal, oil, and natural gas emit different amounts of carbon dioxide per unit of energy produced, measured in kilowatt-hours (kWh). Coal is the most "carbon-intensive" at 0.08 kilograms of carbon per kilowatt hour of energy (kgC/kWh), followed by oil at 0.07 kgC/kWh, and then natural gas at 0.05 kgC/kWh. So, among fossil fuels, natural gas is preferable, as its use leads to less than two-thirds of the emissions from coal. Unfortunately, the trend in the United States has been in the other direction: The decreasing importance of natural gas and the increasing proportion of coal used in the energy mix is one of the factors underlying the country's increasing carbon emissions. This is in marked contrast to what has been happening in countries such as the United Kingdom, where the use of coal, especially in power stations, has dropped sharply and its replacement with natural gas has consequently reduced carbon emissions significantly.

Population and Households

The United States is the third-largest country in the world with a population shortly to hit 300 million. Population has grown considerably and consistently over time: In 1970, the total was just over 200 million. The 1990 to 2000 population increase of 32.7 million was the largest census-to-census increase in American history, and at 13 percent towered over the average of 2.5 percent for other developed countries. In fact, the United States added more people to its population than all other developed countries combined during the decade. This can be explained by two key factors: a high immigration rate and, for developed countries, a relatively high fertility rate, particularly among immigrant communities. Together with rising incomes, the high rate of population growth is a significant driver of increasing energy use in the United States.

Who Uses the Energy and Who Emits Most Carbon Dioxide?

We have seen how much energy is used in the United States compared to the rest of the world. But who is using it and what are the main processes leading to emissions of carbon dioxide from it? While figures for primary energy are required to calculate carbon dioxide emissions, figures for "final energy" are more helpful in understanding where energy is used in the economy. Final energy is the energy actually received by the final user (such as the motorist when he buys gasoline or the householder when he switches on an electric appliance). It differs from primary energy because it excludes what is lost in getting energy to consumers in a form they can use. From this point on in this chapter, all figures relate to final energy, unless otherwise stated.

The proportion of final energy used by different sectors of the economy since 1970 has changed (see figure 6 below). Energy use by industry has become less important, dropping from 44 percent of the total in 1970 to 35 percent in 2003. In 2000, final energy use for transportation overtook that used by industry. Energy use in the transportation sector rose by two-thirds during the period, commercial energy use rose by more than half, residential energy use went up by a sixth, but industrial energy use was the same at the end of the period as it was at the beginning. The proportion of final energy use by the different sectors in 2003 was:

Residential: 16 percent
Transportation: 37 percent
Industrial: 35 percent
Commercial: 12 percent

Within these figures, personal energy use has grown. To get an overall percentage for individuals in the United States, we can take the 16 percent (residential use) and of the 37 percent used in the transportation sector add just over two-thirds of all transportation energy (the proportion not used for freight purposes). The total is more than two-fifths of the economy-wide total. Because of the different fuel types used in each sector, carbon dioxide emissions are not in exactly the same proportions as energy use. In 2003, the residential sector was responsible for 21 percent of emissions, the transportation sector for 32 percent, the industrial sector for 29 percent, and the commercial sector for 18 percent.

RESIDENTIAL ENERGY USE

Overall energy use in the residential sector has increased since 1970. Opportunities to do so in the home have expanded at the same time as the cost of doing so has decreased. Energy prices have fallen relative to incomes: Fuel bills now account for only

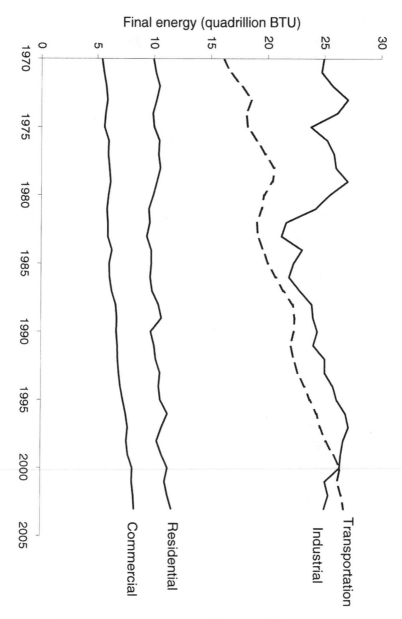

Figure 6: Final energy demand in the United States, 1970–2003. *Source: Energy Information Administration [EIA], Annual Energy Outlook, 2005*

3 percent of the average household budget (although low-income households spend more than 10 percent of their income on energy).

Nevertheless, within the individual household, average energy use has actually decreased over the past thirty-plus years. There have been two opposing trends. Electricity use has increased annually at a rate of around 3 percent. It now makes up almost 40 percent of total energy use compared with only 16 percent in 1970. However, the use of other fuels in the home, mainly natural gas and fuel oil, has fallen by around one-fifth during this same period. Space heating now accounts for around half of the residential sector's use of energy use, compared with two-thirds in 1970. This decline is due to the considerable improvements in the efficiency with which we heat our homes — with wasted heat from inefficient buildings and inefficient heating systems falling significantly. It is primarily these savings that have led to falling energy use per household. Of the other household energy, cooking, lights, air-conditioning, and appliances account for one-third (mainly powered by electricity), and the remaining one-sixth is used for heating water. The proportion and absolute amount of energy used for these purposes has risen.

Both the number and size of households influence total energy consumption in the residential sector. Thus, in spite of the fall in energy use in the average household, the strong increases in population and household numbers have resulted in a sector-wide rise. Household size is important because the same population living in smaller households uses more energy than if living in larger ones. One-person households place particularly heavy demands on the environment, compared with people who live in larger groups. In smaller households — those containing fewer people — the "fixed costs" of energy are shared between fewer people. Each additional household requires its own heating and lighting, refrigerator and television, and, very often, at least one car.

HEATING AND COOLING

The number of locations in which people wish to raise their level of comfort is increasing, expanding from homes, shops, leisure facilities, and places of work, to include cooling in cars (air-conditioning) and heating on patios and in gardens. This rising use of energy for space heating and cooling is resulting in "thermal monotony" — that is, the same internal climate all year round.

Energy use for cooling is a classic vicious cycle, where the response to an issue exacerbates the original problem. As the climate gets warmer, space cooling is sought in more locations, which then requires further energy, thereby adding to global warming, in turn requiring further cooling, and so on, in an upward spiral. Uses for energy-intensive equipment are increasing. In the United States, both ownership and use of residential air-conditioning have been rising over recent decades. By 2001, three in four American households owned air-conditioning systems. The percentage of Americans with central air-conditioning has increased while the ownership of window or wall units has dropped. The proportion of homes with central air-conditioning that report using it "all summer long" increased from a third to a half between the years 1981 and 1997.

While less energy should be required for space heating as the climate warms, more rooms in the home are being heated to higher temperatures for longer periods, and it is not known where these trends will stop. In a household survey in 2001, the average temperature reported in American homes was 70°F. The range was from lower than

63°F in 4 percent of homes, to more than 74°F in 20 percent of homes. As a rough rule of thumb, each extra 2°F requires 10 percent more fuel. If everyone chose to heat their homes to 74°F, energy consumption for space heating would be 20 percent higher than it is today, all other things being equal. Preference for more control of the internal climate is one of the factors leading to increasing disruption of the external climate.

HOME EQUIPMENT

Other changes in the home include wider ownership and, often, more frequent use of dishwashers, clothes washers and dryers, microwaves, televisions, personal computers, CD and DVD players, and other entertainment equipment. Many of these items were rare or nonexistent twenty years ago but are now owned by most U.S. households. In a few cases, however, changes have led to decreased energy consumption: Less electricity is now needed for the lower-temperature wash cycles preferred in clothes washers, and microwave ovens use less energy than do their conventional rivals.

Social changes, as much as new technologies, have also added to energy demand. One cause is that energy use within the home has become more dispersed, with more than one television per household being standard. Many homes have extra — usually older, less efficient — refrigerators that are kept running "just in case" they are needed for parties and other events. Bedrooms now tend to be heated to a similar level as living areas, allowing children and adults to pursue various activities elsewhere in the home. This requires additional energy for heating, cooling, lighting, and use of other equipment.

One problem associated with these changes is the greater use of electricity owing to its versatility. New uses for electricity are easily come by in the electronic age — for household gadgets that are on standby mode. Householders are often unaware that these gadgets are using electricity just by being plugged in. Yet, many television set-tops and cable boxes, for example, use almost as much energy when off as when switched on. Individually the contribution is small, but in aggregate it is considerable. The average U.S. home has around fifty watts of standby, equivalent to a fifty-watt lightbulb operating constantly. This corresponds to 5 percent of the home's total electric bill. In fact, total residential standby electricity in the United States requires all the energy from eight large power plants.

This is particularly serious as, with the current mix of fuels used in electricity generation, it is the most carbon-intensive form of energy available to consumers: Each kilowatt hour of electricity results in more than twice the carbon dioxide emissions than a kilowatt hour of natural gas. Yet, the Energy Information Administration expects electricity for computers and other electronic equipment, household appliances, and gadgets not yet invented to be the fastest growth area in energy demand in the United States over the next twenty years.

TRANSPORTATION AND ENERGY USE

Increasing transportation is a key feature of U.S. society, so much so that its use of energy since 1970 has increased by about two-thirds. People are traveling much longer distances than in the past, partly because they can afford to do so and partly because they have to. Far more use of energy-intensive transportation is now made than in the past. Each person now travels on average more than forty miles a day on land and more than five miles a day by air — about 60 percent more mileage than thirty years ago. Energy use for travel and the carbon dioxide emissions from it have grown faster than in any other sector.

Of long-distance trips made in the United States, 56 percent are for leisure — vacations, visiting friends and family, and outdoor recreation — 16 percent are for business, and 13 percent are for commuting. Distant vacation destinations made more accessible and competition in the tourist industry, combined with more air routes and cheap fares, rapid rail services, cruise liners, and long-distance buses have led to a spectacular geographical widening of destinations. More and more people are able to travel farther, faster, and at less cost, and can treat the world as their oyster. Improving road systems, general ease of travel, and cultural acceptance of long-distance commuting have encouraged people to accept jobs that are increasingly far from home or entail frequent long-distance travel.

Not all additional travel is voluntarily chosen: For example, people may be required to travel farther as a result of a loss of local services, or a manager may be given regional responsibilities as his or her business opens up branches beyond its local base. The growth of opportunities has created a vicious circle — the higher the speed that people can travel and the more distant the available destinations, the greater becomes the demand for transportation and the more damaging are the impacts on the environment. While most of the rise in personal mileage is due to an increase in journey lengths, there has also been some small increase in the number of journeys being made.

Average figures for the level of carbon dioxide emissions for different methods of transportation hide many variations for individual trips (discussed in more detail in chapter 9), which makes comparisons difficult. They are affected by the number of people in the vehicles — whether cars, buses, trains, or aircraft — the energy efficiency of the vehicles, the speed at which they travel, and the type of fuel used. Nevertheless, despite variations between types of transport, the principal contributory factor to any individual's emissions is the mileage traveled.

CAR TRAVEL

There are 225 million cars in the United States, over 40 percent of the world's total. Fifty years ago, there were 40 million. The number has been increasing by approximately 3 million per year. Many of these are four-wheel-drive SUVs, the most fuel consumptive of all passenger vehicles, which until recently accounted for nearly half of all the light vehicles sold in the United States. Around fifteen years ago, the number of light private vehicles overtook the number of licensed drivers and has continued to grow, such that there are now over 1.2 private vehicles for each driver. Car ownership in other parts of the world is also growing but levels are nothing like those in the United States. For example, the current ratio in Western Europe is equivalent to where the United States was in the 1970s.

Since 1970 alone, average annual car mileage per person has increased by half. Over three million Americans are described as "stretch commuters," traveling at least fifty miles each way to work. And a higher proportion of cars purchased are "gas guzzlers." The result of these energy-prolific practices is that, despite a marked improvement in the average fuel consumption of U.S. cars with particular engine capacities, the fuel economy of the average car now in use has hardly changed in the last twenty-five years. Indeed, carbon emissions from the country's use of gasoline in cars exceed those from the entire Japanese economy.

Burgeoning car usage has also encouraged changes in land use and planning, such as the density of residential settlements and the location of facilities. Increasing distances need to be traveled to reach retail outlets, leisure destinations, and so on. With public transportation unable to match the door-to-door convenience of the car, those without one have faced more and more difficulty in accessing everyday amenities.

The rise in the number of people owning and using cars clearly reflects their positive benefits for individuals (personal mobility, prestige, comfort, convenience, and cost). But it is also strongly and increasingly reinforced by external forces in society that have placed car-borne accessibility at the center of land use planning well into the future. This increased car use can be expressed as a number of vicious circles that account for a significant contribution to the excess of carbon dioxide in the atmosphere:

More cars → fewer journeys by other means especially public transportation → reducing public transportation revenues → leading to poorer levels of service → increasing the attractions of the car.

More cars → more provision for motorists of new roads, parking facilities, congestion-relief schemes → more use of cars.

More cars → changing patterns of development to serve car owners → decline of local shops, hospitals, and other services and facilities → increasing dependence on the car.

More cars → more hostile environments for pedestrians and cyclists → further decline of walking and cycling → more use of cars.

More cars → streets more dangerous for children → leading to parents chauffeuring children (and for more years of their childhood) → more use of cars.

Not only are there social, economic, and planning factors that reinforce dependence on cars, there are also psychological factors at work. Research shows that prolonged use of the car results in the owner's greater dependence on it and a decline of knowledge of and interest in alternatives, with the result that a car-based lifestyle becomes an addiction. Very quickly, the car is converted from a luxury to a necessity. A similar process can be seen in the widening role of air travel, discussed later. It is clearly going to be far from easy to reverse this process, particularly in a society with a cultural and historic love affair with the car — and flying! In all these instances, more cars and more flying lead to increased use of fossil fuels and thereby acceleration of the impacts of climate change.

PUBLIC TRANSPORTATION

Public transportation has always been shaped by two often opposing long-term forces: maintaining or improving the quality of service provided, and pressure to control costs against a background of declining passenger numbers and fare receipts. Much of public transit, which includes buses, trains, and ferries, has declined sharply in the United States since the middle of the last century as car ownership has spread. However, in response to a considerable investment in its services, with vehicle miles being roughly doubled in the last thirty years, patronage has improved somewhat in the last few years, albeit with much lower vehicle-occupancy levels. But passenger mileage by public transit, remarkably, accounts for only about 1 percent of the total for transportation. In comparison with the changes in the use of road-based transit, the services of intercity trains and Amtrak have performed relatively well in maintaining their availability and patronage. However, they carry not much more than 10 percent of even that very low proportion of total land-based passenger travel carried by transit.

Despite public transportation's lack of success, it is still commonly seen to be one of the means of dealing with transportation problems, particularly those associated with urban road congestion. The aim has therefore been to increase the number of journeys made by it. However, given its current minimal share of travel, even doubling its use in the future would barely impinge on the extent of car travel. Surveys of the changes that have occurred following major improvements in public transportation show that these bring about a relatively small amount of transfer from journeys previously made by car. Instead, they lead to an increase in the level of use of those already traveling on it. In addition, like new roads, new public transportation services create new demands for travel. Relying on public transportation to solve the problem caused by the continuing high level of gasoline used in cars is unrealistic.

NONMOTORIZED TRANSPORTATION

Walking and cycling have many undisputed advantages. Not only do they generate zero carbon emissions, they are good for health (adults who cycle regularly have a level of fitness equivalent to that of people ten years younger), they do not contribute to air pollution, they are often the fastest method of movement for shorter-length journeys, and they are an important alternative means of travel for children to get about independently. In fact, nearly one-third of the U.S. population are either children above toddler age or adults who, for one reason or another, are without access to a car. Not least for these reasons, the needs of pedestrians and cyclists are important to take into account.

However, both modes have experienced decades of neglect in transportation planning, visible in nearly every city and town across the United States, for example in communities built without sidewalks and roadways with no additional space for cyclists. These two nonmotorized transportation options had been largely overlooked by federal, state, and local transport agencies. In 1990, the Federal Highway Administration (FHWA) described bicycling and walking as "the forgotten modes" of transportation: At that time, an average of just $2 million of federal transportation funds was spent each year on projects to cater for them.

Not surprisingly, census data shows that the percentage of commuter trips made by bicycling and walking has fallen steadily. Walking trips for all purposes account for fewer than one in ten and bicycling for fewer than one in one hundred of all travel trips. It would appear that record bicycle sales in recent years are yet to translate into miles on the road. Overall, walking represents 0.7 percent and cycling 0.2 percent of person-miles of daily travel. Savings of carbon dioxide emissions as a result of a relatively easy transfer from motorized modes of travel for short journeys requires behavioral change that most people appear unwilling to make.

AIR TRAVEL

International and domestic air travel in nearly all countries is of particular concern for four reasons. First, it is highly energy-intensive, using more energy per person-mile than a single-occupancy car. Second, its contribution to global warming is nearly three times greater than is indicated by the carbon dioxide emissions alone. This is due to a number of factors including the warming effects of other greenhouse gases that aircraft release in the upper atmosphere. Third, its speed enables and encourages people to travel long distances. And fourth, its use is increasing rapidly. These factors combined have led aviation to represent by far the fastest-growing source of greenhouse gas emissions. Aviation has a privileged position in the economy: As with car travel, any year in which higher levels of air traffic are recorded is interpreted as "a good year," and encouragement is drawn from any evidence indicating the prospect of more growth.

In the United States, since 1970, air-passenger mileage has increased four-fold to a point at which U.S. airlines use one-third of the world's aviation fuel each year. In 2004, some 1.7 billion people and 35 million tons of freight were transported by air. The average American makes more than two flights a year and flies twice as far as the average European, and the average European flies ten times as far as the average inhabitant of Asia (including Japan). If the rest of the world were to follow the aviation habits of U.S. citizens, the number of planes in the sky would increase twenty-fold.

The demand for increasing international travel is explained primarily by the attractions of widening opportunities for business activity, leisure, and tourism combined with increased personal wealth and the availability of travel options, particularly air travel, at a low price. Travel and tourism is now the world's largest industry, accounting for 11 percent of the world's GDP. Economies in many countries are becoming increasingly dependent on foreign earnings from visitors. Almost without exception, the ecological implications of tourism involving air travel have been overlooked. This willful "turning a blind eye" has elements of black comedy. For example, a writer in a UK newspaper recently advised, with no apparent sense of irony: "Go to the Maldives if you want to see it before global warming swamps the islands."

There is also an increasing number of attractions and activities designed to draw on a wide, international audience. These range from sporting events to environmental conferences. The fact that even environmental organizations arrange such events shows how deeply embedded they are in our current culture. The World Wildlife Fund, for instance, holds conferences each year in different locations around the world, including Interlaken, Indonesia, and Katmandu. The Global Justice Movement attracted forty thousand members to the World Social Forum in Porto Allegre in Brazil in 2002. In some respects, more ironic was the Montreal Conference of the Parties to the

Convention (COP 11) in December 2005. This was organized in order to agree on an international post-Kyoto framework for reducing greenhouse gases: It was attended by ten thousand delegates, the majority of whom participated by traveling from all over the world by air!

ENERGY USE IN INDUSTRIAL AND COMMERCIAL SECTORS

So far we have looked at individuals' direct use of energy in transportation and in their homes. But the energy used in the industrial and commercial sectors, including the public and service sectors, provides the transportation systems that we depend on, heats and lights the shops we visit and the schools our children attend, powers the computers of our banks and building societies, and provides the products we buy and the food we eat.

In combination, the industrial and commercial sectors are the source of half the carbon dioxide emissions in the United States. The largest industrial user of energy is bulk chemicals, followed by metal-based durable and other manufacturing (especially cement), petroleum refining, and paper, food, drink, and tobacco, and nonmanufacturing covering agriculture, coal mining, oil and natural gas extraction, and construction. Since 1970, emissions from industrial activity overall have hardly changed. This reflects changes in the pattern of activity with growth in some parts while in others, notably energy-intensive ones, it has played a declining role. More energy-intensive products are being manufactured abroad and then imported: In other words, energy is being consumed and carbon dioxide emitted on our behalf in other countries of the world. It is therefore important to bear in mind that we do not know precisely whether figures of national emissions represent a true indicator of the "carbon burden" our activities are imposing.

Energy demand in the commercial sector, which includes the public sector, such as schools, hospitals, and local government, is dominated by the energy used in buildings, particularly space heating, air-conditioning, and hot-water provision. Lighting is its largest single source of electricity demand. Its increasing role in today's life is reflected in the fact that, since 1990, carbon emissions from the use of energy in this sector has increased by nearly one-third, so that it now accounts for over 17 percent of total emissions.

On a typical day, about forty-three million tons of goods are carried over an average distance of just under three hundred miles on the U.S. interconnected transportation network. These freight movements have risen by one-quarter in the last ten years. Road and rail accounted for the lion's share of the increase — by 56 percent and 30 percent, respectively. Pipeline transportation, mostly of water and fuel, increased by 27 percent. By contrast, transportation by water — the least carbon-intensive — dropped by 12 percent. Ongoing increases in freight movement, as measured in ton-miles, are explained mainly by longer journeys, with only a minority due to a greater amount of goods being carried. The increase in the average length of journey results from changes in distribution patterns, such as the development of regional distribution centers replacing local ones, and "just in time" deliveries.

These developments in business practice have come about because of the cheapness of road transportation but they are detrimental to both the local and the global environment. Strikingly, a considerable amount of the fuel consumed by the transportation system is used to carry fuel itself to the customers who use it. Indeed, nearly a third of total ton-miles are dedicated to moving petroleum products, coke, and especially coal, principally by rail and truck.

Air freight is the most polluting form of transportation. Originally, it was used only as a means of filling excess storage space in passenger aircraft, but as wider-body planes have been developed, it has increasingly become an important activity in its own right. The tonnage carried by air, taking off or landing at U.S. airports, rose about 9 percent each year in the 1990s, roughly doubling its level to reach about fifteen billion ton-miles in 2003. And the trend is continuing with more freight being moved on longer journeys both within the United States and overseas.

ENERGY USE IN FOOD: FROM FARM TO FORK

The case of food production highlights how ingrained the increased consumption of energy has become in this aspect of our day-to-day lives. The reasons for this range from dietary changes to new patterns of retailing. Even without realizing it, we as consumers are involved in making choices that have a further damaging effect on the climate. The trends and underlying forces behind them can be seen in the United States as in other affluent countries.

TRENDS IN FOOD CHOICE AND COOKING

There has been considerable change in eating habits in the last few decades, leading to a preference for foods that require more energy for production and distribution — at present, about six calories of fossil fuel energy are needed to produce one calorie of food. (A calorie is a measurement of energy usually used for food, but it can be applied equally to any type of energy including fossil fuel.) People are buying fresh and frozen imports of more exotic vegetables. Because these are far more likely to be transported from a distant location, they entail far higher use of energy than food grown within the country. In addition, diet is much less affected by the seasons, as many fruits and vegetables are now available all year round. Though convenient and desirable for consumers, this imposes an energy penalty as they have to be grown either in heated greenhouses or farther afield and again transported, often over long distances, to the retailer and then to the consumer.

Another influential factor is the expansion of the market for convenience foods and ready-made meals, which require more energy in the process of getting them to the consumer. This trend toward convenience foods has been facilitated by two technologies that have developed in parallel: the freezer and the microwave oven. Although the microwave represents a low-energy cooking technology, the use of freezer and fridge space — in transportation from the factory, in retail outlets, and in the home — increases the overall energy used for food storage. Compare energy use in such practices with that of the traditional, fuel-free larder.

GROWING

Conventional farming, particularly meat production, is increasingly energy-intensive. A key reason is that, in contrast to organic agriculture systems, it relies on the manufacture of artificial fertilizers, mainly nitrogen-based, which use considerable amounts of fossil fuel. The differences can be considerable: Organic arable production uses one-third less energy and organic dairy three-quarters less than their conventionally farmed equivalents. Modern, industrialized systems of production, while cost-efficient in commercial terms, often depend heavily on fossil fuel input. Farming is no exception. The foot-and-mouth disease crisis in the United Kingdom in 2001 highlighted the increased movement of livestock, with some animals being taken on eight different journeys between the farms where they were born to the farms at which they would be reared to maturity.

TRANSPORTING

The issue of "food miles" is beginning to attract attention for good reason. Of all consumer products, food is the largest single cause of carbon dioxide emissions. In the United Kingdom, it accounts for more than 30 percent of all road freight and for more than 10 percent of the volume of goods transported by air. Food is now traveling farther than ever before by air, sea, rail, and road. In the last decade or so, food-ton miles rose in the United States by about a quarter. A study of the Chicago market revealed that fruits and vegetables from the production source to the end consumer are typically carried between one and two thousand miles. An Iowa-based study of twenty-eight fresh produce items established that the conventional system led to between five and seventeen times more carbon emissions compared with the regional or local system, owing principally to the additional transport-energy requirements.

RETAILING

The food sector affects energy use because the miles traveled by householders to do their shopping have to be taken into account. Patterns of food retailing have changed considerably in the United States in the last fifty years, with an increasing proportion of people doing their main shopping at malls generally located out of town. Much of their growth was facilitated by the spread of car ownership and planning policies. These policies took insufficient account of the negative effect on local shopping facilities and the problems for those without cars, let alone the environmental consequences. Subsequent patterns of shopping have proved self-reinforcing with greater dependence on superstores, which increasingly consolidate into ever larger and more attractive outlets by offering wider choice and lower prices. This has also enhanced the benefits of having and using a car, not only to carry the larger quantities and weight of goods now bought but to cover the greater distance that typically has to be traveled to reach the stores. In the United States, shopping trips account for about one in five of total trips and for one in ten of all personal mileage. In the last thirty years or so, the average mileage traveled for this purpose has risen by around a half.

Because of their dominance, ways of doing business that suit the retailers influence all the other players in the food chain, including suppliers, farmers, manufacturers, and transportation companies. Their sheer size and centralized organization make it difficult for them to supply locally produced food. While the growth of supermarkets has taken place in response to the preferences of most shoppers, it has also played a major part in the intensification of energy use in the more complex process of getting food from the farm to the home.

WHAT DOES THIS TELL US?

The increase in energy intensity of the food chain over recent decades has not been caused by a single factor. It is the product of many influences, including planning policies, the concentration of retail outlets, changes in production practices, changing consumer tastes, new technologies (such as freezers and microwave ovens) allowing new forms of consumption, declining costs of car and air transportation, and increasing demand for a wider choice of goods from around the world. These changes affect many supply chains. A comprehensive study of the energy used in meeting current patterns of food and drink consumption has been undertaken in the United Kingdom. It indicated that it is by no means insignificant: It accounts for 13 percent of the country's carbon emissions.

In addition, as with other forms of consumption, the energy impacts of food depend on how much is bought. Overconsumption of food in the developed world is reaching epidemic proportions and has a direct, negative effect on personal health and well-being. In the United States, sixty million adults (over one in five of the population) are obese — a clear metaphor in itself for the damage to the planet from our excessive use of energy.

The problems in today's food system are complex, but the alternative is simple to describe. In a less energy-intensive system, food would be more locally produced, more seasonal, more organic, less processed, and purchased closer to home. Achieving this will take time, thought, and effort and will necessarily narrow some aspects of choice. But public policy and consumer practice may well have to be revised to that end.

FUTURE ENERGY USE: LOOKING AHEAD
POPULATION GROWTH

The world's population, economic wealth, and energy use, all of which affect climate change directly or indirectly, are predicted to continue to rise over the next fifty to one hundred years. World population stood at 6.1 billion in mid-2000 and is currently growing at an annual rate of 1.2 percent — an extra 77 million people each year. The midrange estimate for world population in 2050 is 9.3 billion, representing a rise of 50 percent (the lowest projection is 7.9 billion and the highest 10.9 billion). The populations of countries that are more developed, currently 1.2 billion, are not expected to change very much because fertility rates are expected to remain at or below replacement levels. Growth will occur predominantly in the developing countries.

WEALTH AND ECONOMIC GROWTH

Most economic forecasts to 2100 show huge increases in gross domestic product (GDP), the global figure ranging from eleven- to twenty-six-fold, depending on the scenario. If the trend of much higher rates of economic growth in developing countries continues, the income differential per person between developed and developing countries in all the scenarios is expected to fall considerably by the end of the century from the current very unequal ratio of 16:1 to between 2:1 and 4:1. The economy of China, with 1.3 billion people, has been growing at around 8 percent per year since 1980 and is planned to expand four-fold within the next twenty years. Between 1990 and 2100, individual incomes are expected to rise three- to eight-fold in industrialized countries but twelve- to seventy-four-fold in developing countries. These levels of growth are dependent on large increases in the use of fossil fuels and other natural resources. In China alone, over 550 coal-fired power stations are to be built by 2012. According to the World Energy Council, energy use in developing countries will come to dominate world consumption, growing from about one-third of the total in 1990 to almost two-thirds in 2050. Trends in population growth, economic growth, and energy use are discussed below, as are the implications for climate change.

FUTURE ENERGY USE IN THE UNITED STATES

Life in the United States is expected to continue to be more energy-dependent into the future, leading to growth in carbon dioxide emissions. The Energy Information Administration (EIA) produces annual forecasts of energy use and carbon dioxide emissions based on analyzing historical trends and their relationship to factors such as economic growth, fuel prices, and current government policies. The central projection — the "reference case" — up to 2025 — is in effect a "best guess" about what will happen.

The forecasts made in 2005 used actual energy data up to 2003 as their starting point. EIA suggests that total final energy use in the United States will rise by over a third between 2003 and 2025, with an annual growth rate of 1.4 percent per year. Transportation and commercial energy use are expected to see rates above the national average, of 1.8 percent. In the residential and industrial sectors, it is predicted to be about half that, at 0.9 percent. In both the residential and commercial sectors, the most rapid growth is projected to be for electricity used to power computers, electronic equipment and appliances, and telecommunications in the commercial sector.

The overall prediction is that transportation will significantly increase its share of national energy to 41 percent of the total by 2025. Assuming the same share as at present between freight transport and passenger travel, direct personal consumption will then account for 42 percent of the total. The rise in carbon dioxide emissions is projected to exceed that of energy use. This is chiefly because fossil fuel usage is expected to grow more quickly than lower or zero-carbon alternatives — nuclear and renewables — hence increasing the carbon emissions of each unit of energy used. However, it is important to note that many of the factors that affect energy use — such as world oil and gas prices, future government action or agreements that might be taken on energy policy on reducing carbon dioxide emissions, and advances in energy production and consumption technologies — are inherently unpredictable. Moreover, projections do not include international air travel emissions. Therefore, all predictions about the future have to be viewed with a considerable degree of caution.

ENERGY INCREASES: THE HOT SPOTS

Within the generally predicted rise in energy use, there are "hot spots" that could lead to energy use exceeding current predictions. These include changes in population and number and composition of households, higher indoor and outdoor comfort levels, take-up of existing and new uses for electricity, and increases in air travel and car ownership and use.

CHANGES IN POPULATION AND HOUSEHOLDS

Earlier in this chapter, we discussed the expectation that the U.S. population will continue to grow at a much faster rate than that of other developed countries. In fact, the middle forecast is that there will be over 400 million people living in the United States in 2050. However, it is not only the growing population that will drive up the demand for energy. The fastest-growing states in the United States are in the South, where dependence on fossil fuels such as for air-conditioning is much higher than in other parts of the country. There is also the trend for people to live in smaller groups, resulting in smaller household sizes and increasing numbers of households. Since 1970 the average number of people per household has fallen from 3.1 to 2.6; in some parts of Europe, it has already fallen to 2.1. Given its higher fertility rates, household size in the United States is unlikely to fall this far in the near- or medium-term future. However, it should be noted that, as part of the trend to smaller household size, the percentage of one-person households in the United States has already risen sharply from 18 percent of all households in 1970 to 26 percent by 2000.

INCREASING USES FOR ENERGY IN THE HOME

Expectations of rising standards of living, if met, will inevitably result in further climate change. The United States has become a wealthier nation, and the changing attitudes, preferences, and income of its population have led to increasing energy use. It is no longer necessary to live with uncomfortably hot summer temperatures or cold winter temperatures that were previously acceptable. Central heating and air-conditioning will increasingly be taken as an essential component of most households. And yet more energy-guzzling technologies reliant on electricity — ever-larger refrigerator-freezers, several television sets, digital entertainment equipment, and many other gadgets — will also become commonplace. Improvements in energy efficiency cannot keep up with these ever-rising demands.

AIR TRAVEL

Our culture urges us to travel more often and farther both within the United States and increasingly overseas. The travel sections of newspapers clearly show the avenues for future growth: They are full of advertisements and articles encouraging ever more flying — to different parts of the United States and increasingly to far-flung locations in different continents. There is a near-universal collusion in this dream of ever farther and faster travel to exotic locations, promoting the belief that distant travel is horizon expanding, interesting, high status, luxurious, and something to which we can reasonably aspire and, as incomes rise, enjoy. Air travel shows the fastest growth rate in fuel consumption of all transportation modes: U.S. domestic air travel is now increasing at 2 percent per annum and is expected to have doubled by 2020. There is every reason to believe that these trends will continue if no action is taken to curb demand.

Car Travel

Again, our culture urges every adult to buy into the car-dependent culture. In short, the increase in car travel has become self-perpetuating, encouraging people to travel farther and farther. At the same time, it has locked them into an ever more energy- and carbon-intensive way of life — almost to the point of addiction. This no doubt is a major factor behind the prediction that the transportation sector will generate nearly half of the 40 percent increase in U.S. carbon emissions in 2025.

No Shortage of Fossil Fuels

There is a popular misconception that we need to worry about the world running out of fossil fuels. But long before fossil fuels run out, the effect of continuing to use them at current rates will cause havoc to the climate, and that should be the greater cause for concern. Total carbon dioxide emissions from fossil fuel use since 1750 are estimated at 280 GtC (thousand million metric tons of carbon). It has been calcuated that if we used the total remaining reserves on earth, resulting emissions would amount to 5,000 GtC, equivalent to around eighteen times more carbon dioxide than has been emitted over the past 250 years. It is essential that the significance of this calculation be properly acknowledged if disastrous climate change is to be prevented. Governments around the world continue to act as if the exhaustion of fossil fuel reserves is a serious problem when it is the last of our problems. Using even a fraction of what has already been discovered would spell the end of a habitable planet for most of its population.

Conclusions

This chapter has shown just how deeply embedded the use of fossil fuel energy is in all aspects of our lives. Delivery of the unstated goals of society of "bigger and better," "farther and faster," and "more powerful and more widely available" have been achieved through more use of fossil fuels. Predictions assume that it will be possible for everyone in the world to consume more than current U.S. levels. Yet, if people in the developing world had the same energy-intensive lifestyles as those currently enjoyed by people in the developed world — and that is the direction being taken — overall global emissions would now be three times their current level. The finite nature of the planet's resources and its environmental limits make these predictions both fanciful and dangerous because such a level of consumption is obviously unsustainable. Economic growth clearly cannot continue to be pursued as if there were no ceiling on the use of resources or on the capacity of the planet to cope with the consequences of ignoring them.

Nevertheless, if currents trends continue, there are few limits to energy growth on the horizon. Spectacular success has been achieved in finding new ways of using energy, especially for travel over long distances. Electricity has played an ever-wider role in enabling the development and acquisition of labor-saving appliances and leisure equipment, and there will certainly be new, "essential" items available in the future. When demand has exceeded supply, government and industry have combined to provide more of what the public wants, be it more roads or airport capacity and more power stations to ensure "security of supply" — that is, electricity always being available even at peak periods of demand. There seems to be little acknowledgment of a parallel environmental requirement of ensuring "security of climate."

This chapter's main points are:

- Use of fossil fuel energy is deeply embedded in all aspects of our lives and is rising fast worldwide.
- Energy use per person is very unevenly distributed across the world, as are the resultant carbon dioxide emissions and therefore personal contributions to climate change. In the United States, energy use has increased by almost a half and carbon dioxide emissions from burning fossil fuels by over a third since 1970.
- Primary energy use for transportation in particular has grown rapidly owing to rising dependence on cars, far more air travel, and a considerable increase in the distance traveled for all types of journeys.
- Energy use in the residential sector has also risen steadily, due primarily to an increase in the population and more use of electricity for appliances in the home and for lighting. Industrial energy use has varied over time but is about the same now as it was thirty years ago, while energy use in the commercial sector has increased significantly.

We continue to avoid evidence that stares us in the face. Instead of adopting lifestyles based on extreme thriftiness in the consumption of resources, we maintain ones that are resulting in the production of hugely excessive emissions, thereby relentlessly accelerating the process of climate change. In common with other countries in the developed world, the United States is heading inexorably away from a path that would lead to a significantly lower energy economy and drastically reduced carbon dioxide emissions. How responsive will the general public be to the prospect of reversing this trend and beginning to live within the environmental limits of the planet? Chapter 3 looks at evidence on the public response to climate change.

3
Eyes Wide Shut

THE RESPONSE OF
THE GENERAL PUBLIC

Chapter 2 revealed that our lives have become heavily dependent on the use of fossil fuels and that this is leading to a steady deterioration of the condition of the planet. With only a limited planned response on the horizon, there is a distinct prospect of a runaway effect of global warming taking place. The reversal of this process can only occur — as it must, and soon — if the general public passes through four stages to make substantial changes in their lives.

1. Awareness of climate change and its critical link with carbon emissions from our fossil fuel use.
2. Appreciation of its actual scale and the urgency of the crisis that is therefore facing us.
3. Making the connection with their lifestyles and everyday decisions.

4. Responding actively and sufficiently in light of this.

Where are American citizens on the four stages of this pathway today? It is fair to say that most have reached stage 1. Public opinion polls over the last fifteen years or so suggest that they are now at least familiar with the concept of global warming and the causal effect of carbon dioxide emissions. Surveys reveal that two-thirds of the population are mostly or completely convinced by the scientific consensus on this, with little difference between Democrat and Republican voters. Only 6 percent now think that it is not a problem requiring action. Polls also show that the great majority now subscribe to the view that greenhouse gas emissions should be limited and say that they would support legislation requiring large companies to cut their emissions. Three-quarters consider that doing nothing about climate change is irresponsible, with — encouragingly in view of its implications — the same proportion supporting the proposition that a voluntary approach to the reduction of greenhouse gases will not work.

All this is somewhat surprising given the fact that, over the years, public understanding of the issue has been distorted for a variety of reasons. The media are at pains to present a "balance" of opinion or a newsworthy story, and this has led to the views of skeptics being given undue prominence in reporting politically controversial scientific issues such as global climate change. In addition, the government has attempted to limit public exposure to politically sensitive facts even when the source has been its own scientists. James Hansen, the director of NASA's Goddard Institute for Space Studies, a leading climate expert, has accused the Bush administration of trying to prevent him from communicating to the public his grave concern about global warming and the need for immediate cuts in greenhouse gas emissions.

While there has been growing concern among the American public about global warming for several years, the devastating effects of Hurricane Katrina in 2005 acted, to some extent, as a wake-up call. It certainly brought home, with a vengeance, the realization that the populations of affluent countries are not immune to the ravaging consequences of climate change. In particular, it may have sown the seeds of concern that further lethal disasters resulting from rising land and ocean temperatures — the most likely causes — could make the horrors of Katrina appear minor by comparison.

When it comes to stage 2, few people know about the actual scale and timescale of climate change and are therefore unaware of the inadequacy of current national and international policy, particularly in view of the more recent scientific evidence discussed earlier.

So it is a tiny minority who have reached stage 3 — an appreciation of the contribution that their activities are making to climate change. This requires a degree of detailed knowledge about the carbon emissions associated with typical energy-dependent activities. As yet, few are familiar with this. And, whatever the extent of their appreciation of the problem, people, in some respects understandably, see the demands of their everyday lives as having overriding priority on their thinking and actions. It is therefore unsurprising that hardly anyone has moved on to stage 4, translating that essential understanding into the appropriate changes needed in their behavior and lifestyles.

INFLUENCES ON PUBLIC UNDERSTANDING

That so little progress has been made in these stages is easily explained by looking at the extent of involvement of those who influence public opinion on the subject. Government has not provided the information that would alert people to any view other than that the future holds out the prospect of our being able to more or less maintain fairly similar patterns of life to those we have adopted in recent decades. Indeed, it has rarely seen it to be its responsibility to draw public attention to major, possibly intractable, issues of concern lest it is interpreted as being alarmist. Instead, it has preferred to divert attention from them. This has two apparent benefits for government: First, it avoids the short-term risk of being accused of failure in dealing with the issues satisfactorily. Second, it gives the public the impression that everything is under control, thereby enhancing its longer-term electoral prospects.

The relevant professional and academic institutions and consultancies are also involved. More of them now communicate their concerns on the issue of climate change. Working groups are set up to address the subjects of "sustainable development," security of energy supplies, and so on. At the same time, their members accept commissions for work on improving the country's infrastructure, such as for airport design and construction to accommodate growth in air travel, knowing its highly damaging ecological consequences. Given the mixed agendas and accountabilities of these bodies, as well as the media, perhaps the most objective development of policy must come from independent think tanks and possibly from strategists working behind the scenes within the political parties.

There is certainly an urgent need to recognize and highlight some glaring contradictions in public policy, discussed in more detail in chapter 5. These emanate not only from government and industry but from the professions most closely linked to practices that affect climate change. Policies are developed and investments are made to encourage people to travel to airports by public transportation and for their infrastructure to be based on "sustainable" principles to lower their environmental impacts. But, at the same time, a blind eye is turned to the immense ecological damage caused by millions of people flying. Were those who fly to be questioned, they might express concern about climate change and, on current trends, the consequent alarming prospects for their children and grandchildren. However, nearly all of them will either be unaware of or will choose to ignore the personal contribution their flights will have made to accelerating its progress. Their relaxed judgment that the twenty-first century can maintain fairly similar directions to those of the last century is mirrored over and over again and is not countered by realistic government information.

Even those supposedly in the vanguard of calling for an adequate response to global warming, such as the green lobby, advocate remedies that do not sufficiently address the criticality of the problem and the essentiality of having a comprehensive framework for its resolution. They promote the view that citizen action, based on better education and the wider take-up of energy-saving measures, will deliver *in time* the required emissions reduction. This may be well-meaning in its apparent intention of not alarming the public too much about the state of the planet, but to believe that most people will be prepared *voluntarily* to dispense with the attractions of their current lifestyles is fairly clearly wishful thinking.

For their part, the media, television in particular, act to a marked degree as the general public's primary source of information on both scientific and policy-related areas. This means that government's messages about climate change are mediated largely through television, radio, and newspapers. But these forms of communication have been remarkably slow to give appropriate attention and priority to reporting issues of this nature. When they do so, the significance of the link with Western lifestyles and therefore the need for their substantial moderation are rarely made. Moreover, advertising, which is the primary if not the sole source of revenue for media in the United States, acts as a powerful and sustained system of propaganda to promote wasteful and environmentally dangerous lifestyles. As a result, the overall picture that the general public has received on climate change and the impact of carbon dioxide emissions has been unclear and arbitrary. Therefore, it cannot be too surprising that individuals glibly trot out ill-informed statements on the subject, such as:

- The climate has changed dramatically in the past, so why treat any new evidence as proof that human activities are responsible for it this time? Variations in sunspot activity could account for the observed changes.
- Hurricanes are just one of those things that happen from time to time.
- The overall advantages of a warmer,

drier world may outweigh the costs: People may be worse off in the future in Africa and India but better off in Canada and Siberia.

Confusion in the public mind is reinforced by the fact that, in many ways, the media, even the progressive newspapers, fail to make the necessary connections, owing no doubt to a conflict of interest in their coverage of major environmental issues. Reports on their front pages on climate change and the expressions of concern about it in their leader columns are juxtaposed with "travel supplements" and the promotion of flights to distant destinations. By the time readers have reached the back page, they will have read articles on buying shares in airline companies, on the attractions of foreign tourist destinations, and on international cultural and sporting events. And they will have been exposed to advertisements promoting fuel-use-intensive attractions, such as sea cruises, gas-guzzling cars, second homes, and cheap holiday flights to far-away destinations. Yet, the take-up of these offers can only exacerbate the problem.

With such contradictory messages it is understandable that the public has yet to fully accept the seriousness of the climate crisis, let alone to have been galvanized into taking individual preventive action. The media like to feed the public with news that will not distress them and, insofar as taking action is necessary, to propose relatively easy changes, such as small increases in gasoline prices, the desirability of installing better roof insulation, and means of promoting greater energy efficiency. The less alarming the viewpoint, the more the public wants to believe it since it enables them to escape examining or reappraising fundamental aspects of their lifestyles.

Thus, a major reason for so little action being taken on climate change in almost every walk of life both at an individual and collective level is the failure of government, relevant institutions, the media, and the green lobby to alert the public to its awesome realities. In sharp contrast, society has been led to expect at best an ever-rising improvement in its material standards, and if not that, then at least that present standards can be maintained in the foreseeable future.

EXCUSES, EXCUSES, EXCUSES

Even for those members of the general public who are now aware of the gravity of the situation and the need to modify their behavior and lifestyles, there is a further set of barriers to overcome. Individuals escape their responsibilities for doing what they know they should be doing in various ways. Often superficial in nature, they reflect a mixture of contradictory beliefs, expressions of complacency, and conscious and subconscious forms of denial and wishful thinking. They include either a lack of knowledge of the subject or an instinctive desire not to be better informed about it. In turn, this may be the outcome of an innate foreboding of the unwished-for behavioral change that may lie ahead. They are almost instinctively deployed in everyday conversation, reinforced by viewpoints picked up from the media.

Excuse 1: I Am Already Doing My Best

Some individuals are concerned about the issue of climate change but take only minimal action. They console themselves, and claim to others, that "at least I am doing something." They seek reassurance for their largely unecological lifestyles by citing involvement in other limited, marginal, and sometimes irrelevant activities or causes. Typical quotes include:

- I try to use public transportation

whenever I can and never drive to the airport.

- I don't own a car, so I don't feel so bad about flying.
- I am a member of Friends of the Earth.
- My house is well insulated and I use only low-energy light bulbs.
- I compost my kitchen waste and re-cycle all my paper and glass.

Psychologically, they let themselves off the hook with these token gestures and carry on with lifestyles that, in terms of carbon dioxide emissions, are still hugely profligate. Often, too, the finger of blame is pointed at other targets, be they countries, governments, institutions, other populations, particularly wayward individuals — and even animals!

- It's the Chinese we should be worried about: Within a few years their GDP and greenhouse gas emissions will outstrip those of the United States, and look at their population!
- Someone should crack down on intensive livestock farming — apparently methane emissions are as serious a problem as carbon dioxide emissions.

- The problem lies with all these people buying SUVs, Hummers, and other gas-guzzling cars.

Excuse 2: There's Nothing I/We Can Do About It

Others fully understand that climate change may well be catastrophic but argue that the point of no return has already been passed. They claim that it is too late to modify their lifestyles in light of this or else argue that their individual actions will make no appreciable difference to the totality of the problem.

- Climate change can't now be prevented. The melting ice sheets in the Arctic will not refreeze.
- I can't see my friends and family on the other side of the Atlantic without flying. Get real!
- There's no way of getting there without my car.
- It's not that I want to live out in the suburbs but I can't afford to live in the city. In any case, my children's education would get destroyed in those inner-city schools.
- If I don't fly, it won't help: There will just be an empty seat on the plane.

- My life's complicated enough as it is without making it more so.
- It's unrealistic to expect me to make such drastic changes unless everyone else joins in.
- You are probably right about the gravity of the situation. I'll just have to plead guilty!

Excuse 3: It's Not My Problem

Others dissociate themselves from the problems of climate change with real or feigned indifference, often making supercilious comments. This is clearly intended to divert attention from their actions and to relieve them from altering their behavior. In some cases, too, they attempt to devalue the argument by stigmatizing the purveyors of "bad news" as scaremongers, fundamentalists, or even hypocrites.

- We don't have to solve our children's problems — we've got enough of our own.
- Nowadays, you can't enjoy yourself without some smart-ass telling you that it's harmful.
- Why should I worry? I'll be dead by the time it happens.
- Maybe, like the dinosaurs, we are

doomed to extinction. The planet will survive!

- Don't lecture me on lifestyles that are contributing to climate change — you drove here!
- Global warming is a godsend to Cassandra-like alarmists warning of impending disaster!

Excuse 4: There Are More Important and Urgent Problems Now

The need for urgent action on climate change is sometimes sidelined by citing other world concerns or crises — poverty, war, terrorism — which, it is claimed, deserve higher priority. It is also argued that society will be in a better economic position to invest in resolving climate impacts at some point in the future.

- The best way of helping the populations of many developing countries is to provide aid for them so that they can have clean drinking water, modern sanitation, electricity, and better roads.
- Implementing Kyoto at vast cost will only delay the predicted temperature rise for a few years.
- Money would be better spent in promoting economic growth in third-

world countries to enable their populations to afford to build dykes to withstand inundation, as the Dutch have done.

- In any case, we can afford environmental protection only with the proceeds of economic growth.

Excuse 5: Technology Will Halt Climate Change

Many of those concerned about global warming place their hopes on the scope of technological development to solve the problem. It is not uncommon to hear people make statements implying that all that is needed is for government and industry to accelerate renewable-energy developments and energy-efficiency practices, such as the production of more fuel-efficient cars.

- Application of already available, let alone new, technologies could increase many times over the efficiency with which our energy-dependent activities are now carried out.
- Excess carbon dioxide emissions can be dealt with by their sequestration in forests, mines, or under the sea.
- Solar panels covering a small area of Arizona could supply all the world's

electricity.

- Nuclear energy is carbon-free and, in any case, it can only be a matter of time before a breakthrough is made in the development of nuclear fusion.
- In twenty-five years, hydrogen energy will power our cars and we will solve both our oil and climate concerns at one go.

This optimism is widespread. It is shared and encouraged by politicians, the media, and industry and enables avoidance of the radical reappraisal of the direction of current policy that will be needed if technology is unable to deliver sufficient reduction in greenhouse gas emissions. As will be shown in chapter 4, while indeed technology can lower the demand for fossil fuels, its potential contribution in the relevant timescale is limited.

Excuse 6: It's the Government's Responsibility

The last line of defense is that it is unreasonable to expect individuals or even communities to act unilaterally when others around them are proceeding with "business as usual." Rather, it is the responsibility of government to lead and ensure that change occurs. Similar reasoning is applied at the national level when it is argued that a country that unilaterally opts for a rapid reduction of emissions will lose competitive advantage.

- I will cut my emissions if I know that everyone else is doing so as part of a wider plan.
- International consensus is a prerequisite for action, as no country can resolve the problem alone.
- Government must therefore sign up to an international binding agreement to ensure success, and it can take only the necessary steps to set and meet targets under such an agreement.

There can be little doubt that these lines of reasoning are, for the most part, justified. However, in one important respect they are not, for they imply that individuals can exonerate themselves for their inaction. A resolution of the problem is then made more difficult, with government feeling less inclined, particularly in a democracy, to impose an obligation on the public to do things that it has not persuaded them are necessary.

CONCLUSIONS

A wide gap exists between public understanding of climate change and the adequacy of the response to it. This gap reflects a disturbing failure of government to communicate the significance and urgency of the issue. It also reflects an unclear and confusing picture painted by the media, large parts of which are not accountable to the long-term public interest. In a democracy, the change surrounding the critical issue on which this book is focused therefore is highly dependent on a much improved three-way relationship between politicians, the media, and the general public. The media have the central role of alerting the public to the limits of the planet's environmental capacity and therefore the unsustainability of our current lifestyles.

However, government is seen by most people, rightly, to have the primary responsibility in this area. It alone has the authority to decide how serious the issue is and, in light of this, which remedial policies must be adopted. Given the fact that the public is addicted to energy-intensive lifestyles and given the evidence that, at present, it is not prepared of its own volition to give these up to the degree that is so obviously essential, only government can intervene effectively.

Its record on this is the subject of chapters 5 and 6, which look at policy and practice on climate change at all levels of government.

It is clear, too, from the evidence set out in the previous chapters that we cannot continue in a near-universal state of denial, close to collective amnesia, about the significance of climate change. Nor is there any justification for a complacent predisposition to avoid facing reality by burying our collective heads in the sand on this most awesome of issues. Nevertheless, the question remains as to whether a way out can be found to deliver sufficient reduction in greenhouse gases in time to prevent serious damage. The confidence that can realistically be placed in technology to do so is examined in chapter 4.

■ ■ ■ ■

PART II:
CURRENT STRATEGIES

■ ■ ■ ■

4
WISHFUL THINKING
THE ROLE OF TECHNOLOGY

There is widespread hope that technological advance will be the key to reducing carbon dioxide emissions. It is more prevalent in the United States than in most other countries. President Bush has repeatedly stressed the need to shift the debate on climate change away from the imposition of targets aimed at cutting fossil fuel use and toward the development of new technologies that would reduce environmental harm without affecting economic growth. His position is that "new technology can enable greenhouse gases to be reduced while at the same time production and energy consumption can go on increasing" and, in this way, "avoid possible negative economic effects from climate protection measures." Promoting clean technology, on which his administration claims to be the world leader, is seen to be "preferable to the imposition of mandatory greenhouse gas limits."

This chapter assesses the most promising contributions that technology could make to the reduction of carbon dioxide emissions and then goes on to ask whether they will enable us to continue our current energy-intensive lifestyles and increasing dependence on energy. There are three broad ways to reduce carbon dioxide emissions via technology: first, through the substitution of nonfossil fuels, whether renewable energy sources, hydrogen derived from them, or nuclear power; second, by enabling greater efficiency in the use of energy; third, by capturing and storing the carbon dioxide emitted from fossil fuel use to prevent it from adding to concentrations in the atmosphere. While all three have some potential to reduce the damage to the climate from excessive carbon dioxide emissions, each has major limitations, particularly when set against the scale of the reductions needed, the costs of taking them up, and the timescale within which this has to take place.

This chapter is organized as follows:

Renewable energy from:
    water
    under the ground
    waste

biomass

wind

solar

nuclear energy

hydrogen

alternative vehicle technologies (such as electric and fuel cell cars)

energy efficiency

carbon sequestration (the removal of carbon dioxide from the atmosphere)

RENEWABLE ENERGY SOURCES

Renewable energy makes use of natural energy flows and sources in the environment, such as wind, waves, running water, sunshine, and biomass (plant matter), which, since they are continuously replenished, will never run out. Renewable energy emits zero or low levels of carbon dioxide and is therefore an ideal replacement for fossil fuels, if acceptable ways can be found to harness enough of it. In addition, when used for the generation of electricity, there is no problem of dealing with highly toxic waste as there is with nuclear power. Renewables can be used in three fundamental ways: heating, fuel for vehicles, and electric power generation. In output terms, they have not increased much in recent years, although this is likely to change in the coming decades with solar energy, biomass, and wind turbines as the main areas of growth. This section looks at current forms of renewable energy and the technologies with the best prospects in order to see how much fossil fuel energy could be replaced and how quickly this could happen.

In the United States, renewable energy now accounts for around 6 percent of primary energy demand, a similar percentage to what it was in 1970. Sixty percent of the renewables are used for electricity generation, contributing nearly 10 percent of overall electricity generation. The current contributions to electricity generation from all renewable sources are shown in figure 7. The remaining 40 percent of renewable energy is used to produce heat and biofuels.

Each of the main sources of renewable energy is discussed in the following pages, with an assessment of their prospects for more substantial contributions to the national energy supply. At the outset, it is important to note that, in contrast to many European countries, the United States has no national target to raise the contribution of renewable energy to total energy use, though at the state level targets are being set (see chapter 5).

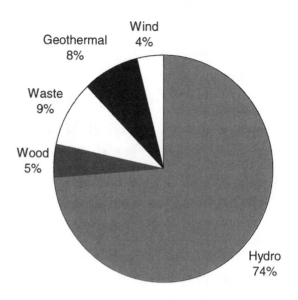

*Figure 7: Percentage of U.S. renewable electricity contributed by different sources, 2004. **Source: EIA, Annual Energy Review, 2004***

ENERGY FROM WATER

Hydropower is currently the most significant source of renewable electricity in the United States, accounting for three-quarters of all electricity generated from renewable sources. Where suitable waterways were found, and hydroelectric plants were built, mainly in the first half of the twentieth century. As most of the best sites have already been developed, there is little prospect of significant expansion in the decades to come. The amount of hydroelectric power available from year to year varies with rainfall patterns. Hydropower has several advantages, not least its relative cheapness. However, there are some negative environmental impacts caused by damming rivers and streams, which can harm the habitats of the local plant, fish, and animal life. In fact, these have been so damaging in parts of the western United States that several dams have been removed recently to replenish ecosystems and restore the natural ability of rivers and streams to transport gravel, sediment, and nutrients.

Investment in research and development into the potential of energy derived from tidal and wave power, notably in Europe, has been made over the last three decades. Although its prospects appear to be considerable given the forces of nature that could in theory be harnessed in this way, only one commercial "wave farm" — off the Portuguese coast — has been built. It remains to be seen whether it could play a significant role in zero-emission electricity generation at a large enough scale and, crucially, at a realistic price.

ENERGY FROM UNDER THE GROUND

Geothermal energy is the heat from under the earth. Its sources range from shallow ground to hot water and hot rock found a few miles beneath the earth's surface, and down even deeper to the extremely high temperatures of molten rock, known as magma.

In the United States, most geothermal reservoirs of hot water are located in the western states, Alaska, and Hawaii. Wells have been drilled into underground reservoirs for the generation of electricity. Hot water near the surface of the earth can also be used directly for heat. Direct-use applications include heating buildings, growing plants in greenhouses, drying crops, heating water at fish farms, and several industrial processes such as pasteurizing milk. Direct use of geothermal energy in homes and commercial operations is much less expensive than using traditional fuels.

Electricity generated from geothermal resources is not yet generally cost-competitive with fossil fuel generation, and its contribution has changed little in recent decades. However, the industry expects electricity generation from this source to increase three-fold over the next twenty years as prices can be brought down below those of fossil fuels.

ENERGY FROM BIOMASS

Biomass energy, or bioenergy, refers to plant material that is used for fuel. The classic energy crop is the tree, but other plants such as grasses are also being investigated. Plants absorb carbon dioxide when growing, and when they are combusted, it is rereleased into the atmosphere. Hence, in theory, there is no net carbon dioxide emission over their life cycle. Most biomass, excluding that grown for fuel, is used to produce heat for the industrial sector. In the residential sector, the most important renewable heat source is wood, though in the United States its use has fallen to around half of its 1990 level. Some biomass is also used to generate electricity. Whether that proves to be cost-effective remains to be seen. In spite of its promotion, its contribution to U.S. electricity supplies has increased by only 1 to 2 percent per annum over the past ten years, though it is planned to double this in the next twenty years.

Biomass can also be used to produce transportation fuels with low carbon dioxide emissions. These biofuels have the advantage that, after being processed, the emissions from them are over 80 percent lower than from gasoline. In addition, the release of acid-rain–causing sulfur dioxide is eliminated. They come in two main types: as biodiesel, which can be used as a direct substitute for fossil fuel diesel, and as alcohol, which can be blended with gasoline in various formulations. Biodiesel is an oil that is extracted from various crops, most commonly rapeseed or sunflowers, and then treated. Alcohol — methanol or ethanol — which outstrips world biodiesel production sixteen-fold, is produced from the fermentation of sugars and starches from various crops including corn and sugar beets. It is a favored additive because it can help reduce local emissions of carbon monoxide in the winter, and because up to 10 percent by volume of ethanol can generally be blended with gasoline without requiring any change in vehicle technology.

One new advance is the biotech development of a genetically modified enzyme that breaks down cellulose into simple sugars. This breakthrough, which requires further refining, allows fuel to be made out of everything from prairie switchgrass and wood chips to corn husks and other agricultural waste. The fuel derived is known as cellulosic ethanol. It has yet to be made in large enough quantities to compete with traditional biofuels, but if the technology works, it could reduce the problem that could otherwise occur as a result of an agricultural landmass being removed from food production. However, although cellulosic ethanol production will not directly compete with food production, it will still affect land use as forest areas come under increasing pressure and may even be replaced with fast-growing monocultures more suitable for the production of this biofuel. The additional pressure could further impair the climate-buffering capacity that these ecosystems provide. Moreover, while there is considerable scope for increasing and developing more efficient ways of producing ethanol and for using more of it in transportation, the entire vehicle fleet would have to be changed to accommodate the new fuel.

ENERGY FROM WASTE

Two of the key sources of energy from waste are incineration of municipal solid waste and use of landfill gas. Landfill gas is formed from decomposing organic material, such as animal and vegetable matter, and paper, which produce gases that are approximately half methane and half carbon dioxide. This source offers a cheap means of generating electricity as it has to be collected for safety and environmental reasons (garbage in landfill decomposes and emits methane for thirty years or more). It can be used to produce electricity, heat, or a combination of the two. Similarly, municipal solid waste can be incinerated with energy recovered either as heat or electricity, or both. Energy can also be recovered by incinerating "specialist" waste, such as tires, plastic, and other oil-derived products. Other waste streams used come from industry, such as forestry, and sawmill wastes, straw, and chicken litter. Much of the debate about this renewable source of energy relates to concerns about the environmental and health impacts of some waste-management options, particularly incineration.

In general, production of energy from waste, whether via landfill gas or incineration, should increase with more waste generation. There is also likely to be further exploitation of sewage gas and waste streams from industry, agriculture, and forestry. But there is a conundrum: By definition, energy from waste requires inefficiencies in other processes. While this book focuses on energy, reducing the use of material resources in general is also a crucial feature of a low-carbon future.

ENERGY FROM WIND

Using the wind for power has had a long tradition in many countries: Look at the eighteenth-century windmills in Holland. Wind is still the renewable energy source thought to have the greatest potential for growth. Since the late 1990s, wind-power production has increased so rapidly that there are now over 50,000 megawatts of wind-energy capacity in the world. This represents more than a ten-fold increase over the last decade and is sufficient to supply the electricity needs of about forty million people.

Some organizations publish very optimistic estimates of the potential of wind power. As the development of wind technology has continued, for example the world's largest — 5 megawatts — turbine began operation in Germany in late 2004, and with new research using lightweight high-carbon blades, the industry's generation of electricity is predicted to increase further. It will particularly benefit from costs coming down in line with an increase in orders and guaranteed quotas having to be delivered by utilities in the future. At present, wind-power generation remains generally more expensive than modern fossil fuel plants.

Wind is the only renewable energy source that has shown strong growth in the United States, with a more than four-fold increase over the last decade. However, this was from a low base. Currently more than 9,000 megawatts of generating capacity, sufficient to produce just 4 percent of renewable electricity, are installed in thirty U.S. states. California, with almost a third of the national total, has the highest capacity, followed by Texas with one-fifth. A typical, modern onshore wind turbine of 1.3 megawatts will produce enough electricity annually for around four hundred average homes in the United States: Supplying one-fifth of U.S. households with wind-powered electricity would require more than fifty thousand additional wind turbines.

The country has a number of prime sites for wind farms, and tapping only a fraction of these would yield considerable amounts of power. According to a study for the Department of Energy, 15 percent of America's electricity could be generated if just 0.6 percent of the land in the lower forty-eight states was developed with wind-power plants. Within that area, as little as 5 percent of the land would be taken up by equipment and access roads: Most existing land use, such as that for farming and ranching, would be unaffected. The Energy Information Administration suggests that given the right policy context, the amount of electricity generated from wind could increase by a factor of ten by 2025, but that in the absence of supportive policies, it would increase only one and a half times.

There is considerable interest in Europe in the potential for wind turbines erected offshore, and a number of offshore wind farms are up and running. The key factor driving this interest is the avoidance of visual intrusion, hence reducing the difficulty in obtaining zoning permits. However, there are significant additional costs of installation and maintenance, including making the turbines robust enough to survive the marine environment and providing undersea cables back to the onshore grid. Typical offshore installations therefore cost twice as much as onshore ones. This can be offset partly by the advantages of their higher wind speeds and more stable wind patterns, leading to higher electricity output, but they are unlikely to fall below those of onshore wind power. The United States has not yet developed any offshore wind farms.

There are, however, problems associated with fully exploiting this renewable source of energy, whether the turbines are onshore or offshore. First, the wind does not blow all the time, and the turbines cannot operate in very low or very high winds. This leads to intermittent generation even with wind turbines distributed across different locations, and this limit therefore has adverse implications on the reliability and stability of the electricity grid. In the longer term, developments in energy storage may reduce the importance of this constraint. Second, power generation varies greatly with wind speed, making relatively high average speeds critical to success. In practice, this often requires the location of turbines in upland, often remote, and visually and environmentally sensitive landscapes. Third, some communities object to having large wind farms in their vicinity on the grounds that they mar the landscape and are noisy. Thus, while wind power is an important resource that should be exploited much more extensively, it cannot in the forseeable future replace the majority of electricity generated by today's fossil fuel power stations.

Energy Direct from the Sun

Currently, there are two main sources of solar power in use in the United States: solar photovoltaics (PV) and solar water heating. Solar photovoltaics turn energy from the sun directly into electricity. Considerable research and development of this technology has been undertaken in recent years. An estimated 1,200 megawatts capacity was installed worldwide in 2004, more than a 50 percent increase on the preceding year. However, this technology supplies just 0.2 percent of U.S. renewable electricity.

PV systems are particularly suited to providing electricity for use in buildings. They can be installed on facades or roofs, and in the sunniest U.S. states a PV roof could supply all a household's electricity needs. It is one of the few technologies available to householders who want to generate their own electricity. However, the key barrier to greater uptake of PV is its high cost: It remains a very expensive way to generate electricity under most U.S. conditions. Official data show that electricity from PV systems costs several times more than conventional electricity despite its cost almost halving since 1990. (The same does not apply in developing countries in areas that lie beyond the reach of the electricity network, where solar PV may be the cheapest option.) On the horizon are new solar technologies, such as the "quantum dots" nanotechnology, improved crystalline silicon and copper alloy alternatives, and thin-film manufacturing processes that may be able to double the efficiencies of future PV systems, further reducing costs and payback times compared with silicon-based PVs. As a consequence, the market for solar photovoltaics could grow significantly, particularly if these developments are supported by federal and state policies. However, at the moment it has limited applications, and its future growth will be largely dependent on continued technological improvements leading to price decreases.

Solar water heating uses energy from the sun to heat hot water in systems of varying degrees of sophistication. Like roof-mounted wind turbines, it can be installed by householders in so called micro-generation schemes. Typically, solar panels for hot-water heating could supply around a quarter of a household's hot water — although in sunnier regions it can supply the majority. It is quite a mature technology but at present its most common application is for heating swimming pools. The key barrier to greater uptake is the initial cost of three thousand to five thousand dollars for the equipment and its installation, with few expectations of significant decreases in price.

NUCLEAR POWER

At first glance, nuclear power appears to offer a source of electricity with negligible emissions of carbon dioxide and on a scale that could eventually replace fossil fuels. While supplies of uranium are limited — potentially just enough for forty to fifty years of supply at current consumption rates — it can be obtained from politically allied countries such as Canada and Australia, giving some assurance of availability over this period. There is also the possibility of extracting uranium from sea water and of using plutonium, via specialized reactors, which can be burned to meet the longer-term demands for nuclear power generation. It is possible that the holy grail of limitless clean energy through the medium of nuclear power based on fusion will eventually be successful. This would sidestep the attendant problems of nuclear fission in that there would not be any shortage of the elements to fuel the process and fewer radioactive waste products. However, despite fifty years of research on this so far, the widely accepted view is that a commercially viable breakthrough is not expected for at least another forty years, if at all.

Nuclear Industry Capacity

The United States is the world's largest user of nuclear energy. In 2005, there were 104 reactors providing 20 percent of the country's electricity supply. However, the expansion of nuclear power has been limited since the Chernobyl reactor explosion of 1986 and the less serious accident at Three Mile Island in 1979, which led to the cancellation of over 100 reactor orders. No nuclear plants have come online since 1996. However, these incidents have not stopped governments and the nuclear industry in recent years from promoting a revived program of construction.

Disadvantages of Nuclear Power

Nuclear electricity is not, as is frequently claimed, carbon-free. Inputs of fossil fuel energy are entailed during the whole life cycle of the nuclear energy process. Fossil fuels are needed for (a) mining and extracting increasingly deep-vein uranium from its ore; (b) transporting and refining it; (c) building the power stations; (d) reprocessing and transporting the waste; (e) decommissioning the power stations; and (f), for an indeterminable time to come, having round-the-clock land and air surveillance to protect against terrorist attacks at power stations and waste disposal dumps. In fact, taking account of all these energy-dependent stages, electricity from nuclear power produces three to four times the level of carbon dioxide emissions from wind generation, though only about one-third of the emissions from traditional coal-fired stations.

The investment required to develop a major nuclear program is vast. Construction costs of power plants are high and have to be repaid with interest, which at current rates accounts for about two-thirds of total costs. The plants have to be decommissioned, but true costs are notoriously difficult to calculate as there is little experience of this or indeed of managing the radioactive waste products for an almost limitless time into the future. Figures released by the International Atomic Energy Agency reveal that the cost of cleaning up the world's existing nuclear waste could amount to a staggering $1 trillion over the next fifty years, with the bulk of that being needed before 2040. It has been calculated that the costs of this for the United States alone will be $400 billion — more than $1,300 for each person in the country — and given the history of cost predictions, these figures may prove unrealistically low. Moreover, running costs have also exceeded predictions: twenty years ago, a number of plants in the United States were retired when it was discovered that it would be cheaper to build and operate replacement gas-fired plants.

The nuclear industry remains optimistic that costs could fall substantially with the advancement of technology despite a poor track record. There have now been decades of government support and subsidies, some of which are hidden and hard to identify: Between 1975 and 2000, industrialized countries spent around $180 billion in today's money on support for nuclear research.

Despite stringent international regulations, the further disadvantages of nuclear power arise from the variety of environmental, health, and safety risks. These include routine releases of radioactive waste from power stations, accidents on site, and the possibility of terrorist attacks. It has been calculated that if an aircraft strike released just half of the nuclear waste stored in one of the Sellafield buildings in the United Kingdom, the release of radioactive caesium 137 would be forty-four times greater than the Chernobyl catastrophe in the Ukraine in 1986. A further risk stems from the potential for the development of nuclear weapons.

A further future risk lies in the fact that nuclear power stations need to be sited near water for cooling. For this reason, some installations are by the sea and therefore susceptible to the sea level rises predicted to occur with climate change. In time, this will mean a huge increase in decommissioning costs as core radioactive material will need to be rescued and plants relocated inland to prevent environmental contamination from their inundation.

Although these are issues of serious concern, the biggest barrier to the expansion of nuclear power is the question of what to do with the radioactive waste products. These require long-term management because some of the hazardous material takes hundreds of thousands of years to decay to a safe state. In order to keep the waste from causing harm to this geological timescale, surface storage — the current interim solution — cannot be seen as a permanent answer. Storage deep in the ground offers an inherently more stable environment with a greater fail-safe capacity and is widely viewed as the only viable long-term option. However, scientific study on storing waste this way is still in its infancy. In the United States, the management of nuclear waste has been repeatedly identified by expert committees and citizens' juries as a problem that must be resolved before the extension of nuclear power can be contemplated.

Nuclear waste also raises the moral question of whether we are justified in leaving a legacy to future generations of large and unknown costs and risks. Many would argue that we are not, and that by using this form of electricity supply to minimize climate change, we are replacing one set of environmental and social risks with another one. Future generations will not have had any input into the decision-making process, so, in effect, we would be entering into a Faustian pact for our benefit but at their expense!

HYDROGEN

In many respects, hydrogen is the ideal fuel. The energy released per ton in combustion is more than twice that of any hydrocarbon, and there are no carbon dioxide emissions as no carbon is involved. It can be stored fairly simply, holding the energy until it is needed, and used as a portable fuel for internal combustion engines. Neither of these advantages apply, to anything like the same extent, to electricity. But hydrogen does not exist abundantly in nature. Like electricity, it is an energy carrier rather than a primary fuel and is only as "carbon free" as the energy used in its production.

There are three main ways of producing hydrogen:

1. Separating it from hydrocarbons chemically, such as methane (natural gas).
2. Using electrolysis to split water into hydrogen and oxygen.
3. Manufacturing it biologically.

The world's chemical industries already produce hydrogen from hydrocarbons but the process inevitably results in carbon dioxide emissions. However, using electrolysis, *if* the electricity is derived from renewable sources — a big *if* — carbon emissions can be truly zero as water is the only by-product. A future, somewhat visionary, scenario could be to cover areas of the countryside with solar panels generating electricity that in turn could be used to produce hydrogen to be compressed or liquefied and then transported to consumers.

Hydrogen can also be produced by photosynthesis or fermentation. Although algae give off only small amounts, a metabolic "switch" has been found in these primitive plants enabling the energy they derive from sunlight to produce the gas. It is just possible that means will be found for this to occur on a large scale by growing algae in mass cultures in tanks, ponds, or the open sea. Research is also progressing on bio-hydrogen production through a fermentation process using starch-rich wastewater as feedstock, thereby potentially offering a cheaper fuel than gasoline. However, research on these alternatives is at the developmental stage.

USING HYDROGEN

The most promising use of hydrogen is for transportation, particularly in cars and other road vehicles. If it is presumed that hydrogen could be produced using zero-carbon electricity for use in road vehicles, two key challenges still remain: distribution and on-vehicle storage. While its energy content on a mass-for-mass basis is better than gasoline, hydrogen is more difficult to transport and store because it is a gas, not a liquid. A hydrogen-gas fuel tank containing a store of energy equivalent to a gasoline tank at atmospheric temperature and pressure would be more than three thousand times larger than the gasoline version. So hydrogen has to be stored in compressed or liquefied form on the vehicle and when transporting it to filling stations. Several technical hurdles would have to be overcome for this to be easily and economically achieved. Alternatively, hydrogen could be created on board the vehicle from natural gas using a "reformer." But, compared with conventional vehicles that run on gasoline, this option offers little advantage, as carbon dioxide would still be emitted.

At present, hydrogen is used as a fuel in just a small number of demonstration projects. Major technological advances and infrastructure changes would be required for it to replace a significant amount of fossil fuel use in the United States. Moreover, there is little prospect of using it as an alternative to kerosene or jet fuel because liquid hydrogen requires around four times the storage space of the fuel now used in planes for the same energy content.

ALTERNATIVE VEHICLE TECHNOLOGIES

There are a number of alternative vehicle technologies that may offer ways of reducing carbon dioxide emissions. These include electric vehicles, "hybrid" electric vehicles, and vehicles powered by liquid petroleum gas (LPG), natural gas, or fuel cells. The interest in these alternatives is in part a response to the fact that the opportunities for increasing the efficiency of conventional vehicles, while retaining their current size, power, and features, are limited. However, research is also motivated by other considerations, such as concern about local air quality, which is affected by pollutants in car exhaust fumes, especially particulates and sulfur and nitrous oxides.

ELECTRIC VEHICLES

Electric vehicles have been under development for more than a hundred years, yet the same major disadvantage — not being able to travel very far on a single charge — has persisted despite improvements in battery technology. They are also unable to deliver similar speeds and levels of acceleration to those of most cars today. Given current performance expectations, these are serious barriers to their greater uptake.

Furthermore, the contribution that electric vehicles could make to reducing carbon dioxide emissions depends on the means used to generate the electricity used to charge their batteries. An electric vehicle using conventionally produced electricity in fact increases emissions compared with an equivalent petroleum-fueled car. Renewable sources would be needed for a "zero carbon" outcome, but current supplies are far too limited for them to be used for transportation purposes. The best prospect for electric vehicles remains as urban conveyances for short journeys made at low speed.

HYBRID ELECTRIC VEHICLES

Much more promising are hybrid vehicles. These have both a fossil fuel internal-combustion engine and an electric motor powered by batteries: The car automatically switches between them depending on driving speed and the extent to which the battery is charged. Different levels of hybridization have been developed, ranging from simply capturing energy lost during braking and returning it to the battery (regenerative braking), to full hybrids, which allow periods of electric-only operation. The electric fuel system is used at speeds lower than 10 mph and for stop-start driving, and gasoline is used to travel at higher speeds. The energy efficiency of the car increases with the degree of hybridization, with up to eighty miles per gallon being possible in a mid-size car with full hybrid features. Compared with equivalent gasoline cars, this represents a substantial saving of fuel and therefore of carbon dioxide emissions. Further progress on the energy efficiency of hybrids can be expected as more research is conducted.

Several hundred thousand hybrid cars are in operation around the world, mostly in the United States and Japan, where they have been developed partly in response to government targets for less-polluting vehicles. Japanese car sales dominate this market and a prediction has been made that a significant proportion of the U.S. automobile market will be hybrids in twenty years. However promising the prospects for their improvement and uptake, vehicles using this advanced technology currently are relatively expensive. Moreover, the batteries required for full hybridization at present take up considerable space, sometimes turning the vehicle effectively into not much more than a two-seater.

Fuel Cell-Powered Vehicles

Car manufacturers are also investing in research and development on fuel cell vehicles and there has been much hype about the combination of the fuel cell with the use of hydrogen. It is claimed that in the long term, renewably produced hydrogen could allow road vehicles to operate with zero emissions. Fuel cells could indeed provide energy cleanly and efficiently. Like batteries, they produce electricity by converting energy directly into usable electric power by a chemical reaction. Unlike a battery, a fuel cell has an external fuel source, typically hydrogen gas. Inside most fuel cells, hydrogen from a fuel tank and oxygen from the air combine to produce electricity and warm water. Fuel cells are efficient, portable converters of fuel to electricity, capable of turning 50 to 70 percent of the energy in hydrogen fuel into electricity.

The advantage of fuel cells depends on how their fuel is supplied in the first place. There are three main routes, listed in descending order of impact:

1. Pure hydrogen produced by using renewable energy.
2. Pure hydrogen produced by using fossil fuel energy.

3. Using a fossil fuel to create hydrogen on board the vehicle.

Only the first offers zero emissions, but, as has been noted, this will not be a realistic prospect in the next thirty years. The two other options offer smaller but important advantages over conventional vehicles. Using fossil fuels to power a fuel cell could offer the same scale of emissions reductions as a hybrid electric vehicle — that is, 50 percent or more. However, even if the technology proves successful, as seems possible, fuel cell vehicles could still not be expected to form a significant proportion of the vehicle fleet for many years.

ALTERNATIVE HYDROCARBON VEHICLES

The popularity of both natural gas and LPG as alternatives to gasoline and diesel in a conventional engine has been growing. Because natural gas has to be compressed or liquefied for use in engines, it requires a bulky storage tank to keep it in this state. For this reason, it is unlikely to be used in cars. Most natural-gas vehicles are heavy-duty trucks and buses, for which larger and heavier fuel tanks pose less of a space or weight problem.

The use of LPG or natural-gas vehicles

offers local air quality benefits, but neither provides better carbon savings than a switch to diesel. Taking account of greenhouse gas emissions per mile, on a "well to wheel" basis that covers all stages of fuel extraction, processing, delivery, and usage, emissions from LPG vehicles and from natural-gas vehicles are about 15 percent and 25 percent lower respectively than from the gasoline equivalent. Ordinary diesel-fueled vehicles generate emissions around 20 percent lower than the gasoline equivalent.

ENERGY EFFICIENCY

Energy efficiency is regarded as a good thing by economists, engineers, and environmentalists alike. It offers reduced use of fossil fuels through technological improvement without business practices, behavior, or lifestyles having to change. It represents a win-win solution with better outcomes for both the consumer budget and the environment. Although less glamorous and less visible than renewable energy, it is a major focus of energy policy. In theory, it has much to offer and there is plenty of evidence to show that it achieves a lot of what it promises. But a fundamental concern from a climate-change perspective is whether greater energy efficiency translates into overall energy savings.

There is a range of views on the scope for improvements in efficiency. Some commentators are extremely optimistic: Books have been written about both Factor 4 and Factor 10, offering the potential of a four- and even ten-fold increase in the efficiency with which energy and other material resources are used. But even the less optimistic would agree that, despite decades of efficiency improvement, there are many existing technologies that have not been taken up. The greatest challenge appears to be not just to develop technology further but to ensure that the most energy-efficient products and processes are actually taken up.

Residential Sector

Considerable increases could be made in energy efficiency in U.S. households, particularly by upgrading the building fabric of poorly insulated, older properties and the equipment used in them. Consumption is determined by how effectively homes retain heat, by the heating and cooling system used, accounting for most of the energy used, and by the energy efficiency and extent of use of appliances. The indications are that a vigorous policy of much higher mandatory standards and better labeling of products, combined with public and private investment in the take-up of cost-effective technologies already in the market, could lead to considerable savings.

Examples of past improvement include much increased efficiency of furnaces, which has led to the average new home built today requiring a third less heating energy per square foot than a home built prior to 1970. Major advances have also been made with air circulation systems, refrigerators and freezers, washing machines, and dishwashers — responsible together for about 20 percent of energy bills in U.S. households.

Making new housing highly efficient — a comprehensive approach can lead to a 50 percent reduction or more — is an important objective. However, reducing energy use in new homes will have a limited impact on the overall energy used in housing, given the large number of existing homes. Reducing energy demand for heating and cooling in existing homes in the United States, the majority of which will be standing for decades to come, will be far more costly than doing so in new homes. Also, it is not generally possible to upgrade old homes to as high a standard as new, superefficient homes. So the savings that efficiency can deliver for space heating and cooling, while considerable, are limited by the poor design and build of the existing homes. In addition, the most cost-effective opportunities for savings become progressively difficult to achieve over time as the most efficient equipment now on the market, such as washing machines and gas furnaces, will be hard to improve upon to any marked degree.

Energy efficiency does not inevitably lead to energy saving. It can lead to higher standards of comfort being adopted. Reducing energy costs through efficiency can contribute to broadening expectations and generating "needs" that did not previously exist. Heating the whole house, rather than just the living areas, has become common practice because of the availability of more efficient central heating systems and better-insulated houses. In this, energy efficiency is part of the broader technological and economic advance that is bringing energy-using equipment within reach of most U.S. citizens. None of this, of course, invalidates the case for promoting energy efficiency in the home, but can guarantee overall energy saving only as an end result where that is an explicit goal.

TRANSPORTATION SECTOR

Energy use is rising most rapidly in the transportation sector, despite considerable improvments in the more efficient design of conventional vehicles. Transportation efficiency can be measured in three ways.

1. Vehicles: the efficiency of moving the vehicle around, measured in miles per gallon of gasoline.
2. Passengers and freight: the efficiency of moving passengers or goods around by each mode of transportation, measured in energy per passenger-mile or, for freight, per ton-mile.
3. Journeys: efficiency as reflected in the amount of fuel required.

Vehicle efficiency is the easiest of the three to measure and can be used to set improvement targets for manufacturers in terms of miles per gallon of fuel. Passenger/freight efficiency is perhaps a more useful measure because it includes more of the complexities of transportation systems, such as public transportation vehicle occupancy rates or truck-loading rates. Finally, journey efficiency captures another important determinant of energy used in transportation in that how efficiently it is used on a particular journey depends on the vehicle used. A change from cycling to school to taking the bus represents a reduction in journey efficiency because the traveler has changed from a personal (renewable) form of energy to one using fossil fuel.

The benefits of improved car efficiency from a national energy-saving perspective depend on the replacement of millions of vehicles. More efficient vehicles take many years in development and construction even before they are first available on the market, let alone in sufficient numbers to make a significant difference to the overall use of fossil fuels. Care must also be taken in using energy efficiency to measure energy savings, as any comparison of the energy used for transportation must also look at energy use per passenger-mile or per ton-mile of freight rather than per vehicle.

Since 1970, average fuel consumption of cars with similar performance characteristics has fallen by 40 percent. However, the benefits can be offset by people buying larger, higher-performance ones with higher energy consumption and energy-hungry features such as air-conditioning. And this is what has happened to a marked degree, with the result that the overall efficiency of the *average* gasoline car purchased has not improved over the past fifteen years. In addition, as car ownership has increased, car occupancy levels have fallen. Thus, energy consumption per passenger-mile has increased and passenger efficiency has decreased. Furthermore, as a result of changes in the travel patterns of the U.S. population cited in chapter 2, any transportation-efficiency gains of recent decades have also been massively outweighed by the increasing use of transportation.

In contrast to this in the field of air travel, the efficiency of aircraft has improved, as has their passenger efficiency (i.e., less energy is used per passenger-mile). However, the efficiency benefits have been completely outweighed by the increase in flying, leading to strong growth in energy use.

CARBON SEQUESTRATION

Carbon sequestration is the permanent removal of carbon dioxide from the atmosphere so that it no longer contributes to the greenhouse effect. There are two forms. First, there is biological sequestration — i.e., growing trees and other plants and organisms that absorb carbon dioxide from the atmosphere and incorporate the carbon within their own molecular structure. The second form uses industrial processes to capture carbon dioxide and to then compress and store it underground or under the sea — known as "carbon capture and storage." This fundamentally different approach has the attraction, particularly for fossil fuel companies, of seemingly maintaining their energy markets while meeting targets for carbon reduction.

BIOLOGICAL SEQUESTRATION

Creating or restoring forests by planting trees has been powerfully symbolic of environmental improvement for many years and has therefore attracted considerable political and commercial interest. In the global carbon balance, forests, together with other natural forms of absorption of carbon dioxide, play a key role.

- As carbon reservoirs: Global forests contain around four-fifths of the carbon stored in land vegetation, the majority of it in tropical forests and the rest divided between temperate and boreal forests.
- As carbon sinks: A natural process by which forests as well as seas and soils currently absorb a significant propor-

tion of the carbon dioxide emitted by burning fossil fuels. (Recently, disturbing evidence has been found of carbon dioxide emissions *from* soils, forests, and oceans, suggesting that some of these sinks may have reached capacity.)

- As carbon sources: When the reservoirs or sinks are depleted through deforestation, mainly in tropical regions, when trees are cleared for growing crops or rearing cattle, and through loss of land to urban and industrial uses.

The land surface available for forestry growth and restoration in the United States and in many countries around the world is considerable. However, planting trees to offset the carbon dioxide emissions from burning fossil fuels has serious limitations. A forest will absorb carbon dioxide as the trees grow but eventually the growth rate and absorption slows until, in a fully mature forest, the rates of growth and carbon sequestration are close to zero. Old trees then die and release their carbon back into the atmosphere as carbon dioxide. A mature forest must therefore be protected not only from fire and pest attack and from too high temperatures and prolonged drought — both of which are likely in a warming world

— but it must also be maintained in perpetuity. From this perspective, the first priority must be to try to prevent further destruction of current forests, such as in the Amazon, a complex political issue that has defied resolution despite considerable international effort over the years.

The relevance of these considerations is revealed by applying the findings of UK-based research on the absorption of carbon dioxide by trees to determine the scale of new forests that would have to be planted for the U.S. population to become carbon-neutral. This calculation shows that at an average annual rate of sequestration over the period from establishment to the old-growth phase (perhaps one hundred years), two hectares of land would have to be planted and maintained permanently in order to absorb the annual emissions from the use of fossil fuels by the average American citizen. At around three tons of carbon per hectare, the U.S. population would need an additional 500 million hectares of permanent forest to what already exists. That is equivalent to more than half the area of the United States! In plain language, planting trees may not lead to significant or permanent carbon dioxide removal from the atmosphere and cannot be undertaken on the scale necessary.

A further problem identified with this route of sequestration has been revealed in recent research at the Max Planck Institute in Germany. This has identified the fact that plants and trees produce significant amounts of methane not just when they rot but during their lives and that this phenomenon could account for 10 to 30 percent of the world's emissions of this powerful greenhouse gas. This study highlights the extreme complexity of the relationship between the biological processes of the earth, the chemistry of the atmosphere, and how much there is still to understand about natural processes affecting the state of the planet. It reiterates the uncertainty about how effective trees can be in mitigating climate change.

CARBON CAPTURE AND STORAGE

Carbon capture and storage consists of capturing carbon dioxide, then compressing and transporting it to an underground reservoir. The carbon must be captured at points where large quantities are produced — most obviously at fossil fuel power stations. The idea of abstracting power station exhaust gases has been considered since the 1970s, but it is only in recent years that government and industry have pursued the idea seriously. Capture of carbon dioxide in this way is now a well-established technology. When account is taken of the energy entailed in the process, it can achieve an overall reduction in emissions of about 80 percent compared with the same power plant without carbon capture. But there is a further input of energy required to compress the gases and then to transport them.

After capture, compression, and transportation, the final stage involves storage in large natural reservoirs that currently contain salt water (saline aquifers), salt (salt caverns), or former gas or oil fields or coal mines. There is only one industrial-scale example in the world of this technology being used at present. Over the last ten years, about one million metric tons of carbon dioxide has been injected into an aquifer formation below the bed of the North Sea off the coast of Norway. This represents about 3 percent of that country's carbon dioxide emissions for one year. Presuming that a substantial number of sites can be found and that the total process proves to be cost-effective compared with other means of controlling emissions, the key risk is of the carbon dioxide eventually seeping to the surface through unexpected pathways, such as old drilling holes or natural faults. Given the asphyxiant properties of carbon dioxide, most suitable sites are likely to be below the sea. Unlike nuclear waste, carbon dioxide does not become less dangerous with time, making the reduction of leakage risks critical to the viability of this technology.

If there were an absolutely reliable way of sequestering carbon via capture and storage, it would open the way for continued use of fossil fuels. In particular it would allow coal, of which there are vast stocks around world, including in the United States, to regain its place as the primary source of energy for the future. However, research has raised questions about the cost-effectiveness, safety, and permanence of the process.

FUTURE PROSPECTS

Having reviewed the potential ways of applying technology and their limitations, the question that must be answered is what are the realistic prospects of their making a significant contribution to reducing emissions of carbon dioxide.

By 2050, renewable sources could contribute far more to the U.S. energy supply, particularly if economies of scale can be made. However, they are likely to represent only a small fraction of the huge reductions required in carbon dioxide emissions. The best prospects with the fewest technical, economic, and environmental obstacles to overcome lie with wind turbines and waste materials for the generation of electricity, and solar panels for water heating. Left purely to the market, little additional renewable energy would be employed for electricity generation or other related purposes simply because, as in the case of photovoltaics (PV), it is currently relatively expensive. Of course, if the full environmental costs of using fossil fuels (including oil spills, local air pollution, and climate change) was charged to their users, renewable energy would be seen to be relatively cheap. The prospects of biofuels as a substitute for petroleum rest heavily on the logistics and costs of having a new generation of vehicle that can run on them and the associated nationwide stations to supply them.

The future of renewable energy therefore depends very much on government policy, which is discussed in the following chapters. Of course, the easiest way of increasing the *proportion* of our energy requirements from renewables — and at no cost — would be to reduce energy consumption! In an ideal world, with better storage systems and much lower levels of demand through improved efficiency and changed lifestyles, renewables could supply the majority of our needs.

NUCLEAR POWER

The case for a major role for nuclear energy as a source for generating electricity is highly problematic. Although its revival is currently a major focus for political discussion and review, the industry's promotion of it as the "carbon-free" answer to climate change is far from accurate. Even in the unlikely event of nuclear power providing 50 percent of U.S. electricity, that would account for only about one-tenth of the country's final energy consumption. Moreover, the risks and high costs associated with it, as well as the unresolved problems of nuclear waste disposal and the moral issues surrounding that cast considerable doubt on its suitability as a means of combating climate change. Proponents of the nuclear option increasingly argue that the consequences of climate change getting out of control make those associated with any realistic risks from failure of a nuclear-based strategy pale into insignificance. Nevertheless, for all the reasons noted, a major program of construction of new nuclear power plants in the next decade or two seems improbable unless governmental priorities change considerably, large amounts of subsidy can be provided, the morality issues can be set aside, and the public can be convinced of the case for it — four unlikely prospects.

Hydrogen

At present, hydrogen is used as a fuel in just a small number of demonstration projects. In the longer term, hydrogen produced from renewable sources could replace other fuels, such as natural gas in the home, and allow road vehicles to operate with zero "well to wheel" carbon dioxide emissions. Research on hydrogen power and associated technologies will no doubt improve its prospects. However, it depends on a surplus of electricity generated from renewable sources if it is to be carbon-free. Major technological advances and infrastructure changes would be required for hydrogen to replace a significant amount of fossil fuel use in the United States. As this is unlikely for several decades, any contribution it can make will be far in the future.

ALTERNATIVE VEHICLE TECHNOLOGIES

Electric vehicles are unlikely to constitute a mass-market solution to reducing the use of fossil fuels for the foreseeable future, owing to the insufficiency of available electricity from renewable sources. LPG and natural gas offer relatively small savings compared with diesel-powered engines. Even if the technology proves successful, fuel cell vehicles could not be expected to form a significant proportion of the vehicle fleet for many years. The most promising near-term technology is the hybrid electric vehicle, which already has proven carbon-saving advantages over conventional ones.

VEHICLE EFFICIENCY

Considerable scope exists for saving energy both by improving the efficiency of vehicles and by ensuring that vehicles are better matched to what they are required to do. In Western Europe, the average fuel efficiency of automobiles is about 50 percent higher than of those in the United States, and a voluntary agreement with motor manufacturers covering the period from 1995 to 2008 is scheduled to reduce the fuel consumption of the average new car by 25 percent.

Further improvements are possible in passenger and freight efficiency by raising occupancy levels of cars and minimizing the "empty running" of trucks. Greater efficiency in aircraft is also in prospect, both through their design and through raising seat-occupancy rates. A 50 percent reduction in fuel consumption per passenger-mile over the next twenty years is widely viewed as feasible. In all instances, however, the likely improvements will not lead to overall energy savings if the predicted parallel growth in demand for travel is realized.

Energy Efficiency in the Home

Improving energy efficiency is probably the most effective approach to reducing carbon dioxide emissions, and many opportunities exist for improvement. Many of the savings can be made with little or no investment of capital as they rely on improved housekeeping, better control of existing systems, purchasing the most efficient version of household equipment on the market, and applying better technologies and management systems. With new housing, the energy demand for heating and cooling could be dramatically reduced: Minimum standards can be raised through updated and enforced building codes, while new mechanisms will have to be found for upgrading existing homes and for financing improvements, in some instances subsidizing them. But for this to occur, more vigorous, comprehensive, and better-funded energy efficiency programs than exist at present are required.

The scope for applying efficiency measures in all sectors of the economy is considerable, but there are boundaries — and take-up has a poor track record. In addition, improvements in efficiency do not necessarily lead to energy savings. In the residential sector, overall savings will not be achieved against a background of increasing population and household numbers and continued growth of energy-based activity and the very powerful forces promoting it. As a result, energy use in this sector is expected to be higher in 2020 than today, even with efficiency improvements.

CARBON SEQUESTRATION

Carbon sequestration can make only a small and in all likelihood unreliable contribution. It represents a highly attractive technical fix that could in theory enable our current carbon-intensive lifestyles to be maintained. However, in the case of afforestation, totally unrealistic areas of land would have to be planted each year and the trees would have to be continually replaced when they died. In addition, the carbon balances of forests, particularly under a changing climate, are uncertain. This means that the number of trees to look after would rise yearly in order to continue to store in them all the carbon dioxide from the use of fossil fuels in previous years. In the case of carbon capture and storage, even setting aside the high costs entailed in the process, safe storage underground would have to be totally reliable over the very long term — an extremely difficult condition to meet.

SUMMARY OF TECHNOLOGY-BASED FORECASTS

Several studies have been carried out to estimate the reduction in greenhouse gas emissions by applying these promising technologies. A comprehensive analysis of clean energy futures prepared in 2000 showed that even with the aggressive deployment of many of the technologies described above, less than a 12 percent reduction in greenhouse gas emissions compared to 1997 levels was conceivable by 2020. A more recent Tellus Institute study that included carbon sequestration, the full deployment of hydrogen for road transportation, aggressive efficiency programs and the widespread use of renewables resulted in predicted 2050 emissions that were about a third below 2000 levels. Unfortunately, even this herculean exercise in technological optimism results in reductions of greenhouse gas emissions that are woefully inadequate.

CONCLUSIONS

This chapter has presented an overview of the three carbon-reducing options: using less carbon-intensive energy, making more efficient use of energy, and capturing and storing the carbon dioxide emissions from using fossil fuel energy. It has led us to the conclusion that technology alone cannot provide the high level of reduction of emissions that are urgently required. This is especially so given the wide range of problems and uncertainties associated with the options described, including time and cost constraints. For example, renewable energy sources are currently limited, relatively expensive, and are almost nonexistent for heating and transportation fuels. It would be wishful thinking to believe that the application of technological fixes will enable life to go on more or less as we know it.

We do not suggest that technology cannot help reduce the impact of energy use. But in our view it cannot play a crucial role in mitigating climate change in a business-as-usual world where forces for energy-dependent growth continue to dominate. The idea that "every little bit helps" is a dangerous one. Even the combined and most optimistic projections of technological developments will not begin to deliver the reductions required. Only in the context of strict limits on carbon dioxide emissions can the technological options discussed in this chapter play a meaningful role in averting climate catastrophe.

5
FIDDLING WHILE ROME BURNS

WHAT GOVERNMENT IS DOING TO REDUCE FOSSIL FUEL DEPENDENCE

Can we carry on with our lives as usual and leave the government both at federal and state level to deal with climate change? This chapter argues that the answer to this question is an emphatic no. Some U.S. states have taken steps to promote energy efficiency and renewable energy in an effort to address the problem. But the federal government has not, and is dangerously resistant to taking any significant steps in that direction. Furthermore, not even the most environmentally progressive state governments seem prepared to tell voters what they do not want to hear, namely that dramatically reducing carbon dioxide emissions requires significant lifestyle changes as well as making the best use of technological advances. In order to guarantee the necessary progress toward reductions in emissions essential to the survival of the planet, this apparently unpalatable truth must be faced.

What is the U.S. government doing and what does it propose to do to move toward a low-carbon future? After all, it is its job to provide collective goods such as national security, clean air, a social safety net, and protection of the environment from catastrophe. Leadership and commitment at the federal level has to be provided to reach this goal, even though that can be achieved only in cooperation with civil society and business interests and, more widely, through agreement with other countries. For this process to be successful, radical changes are required.

Government policies and responsibilities specifically, and society's responsibilities more generally, are at the heart of the matter. Looking to government policies cannot mean ignoring the role of individuals. Government is influenced by them directly in their role as voters as well as indirectly through their representatives and their membership in special interest groups (such as the Automobile Association of America and the Sierra Club). So, while this chapter is about government actions, it is also about what citizens and voters should encourage it to do and seek to prevent it from doing on their behalf.

What Should Be Happening

While still enjoying as many of the benefits of energy use as possible, society, we believe, should be aiming to make the necessary changes that will assuredly reduce carbon dioxide emissions to the extent that climate science indicates is essential. To that end, we put forward the following steps that need to be taken, in order of priority and importance.

1. Achieve massive reductions in energy-dependent activity.
2. Ensure that the energy still required is used as efficiently as possible.
3. Supply as much of it as possible from low-carbon and renewable sources.

The essential difference between our position and that of even those state governments that are doing something about climate change is step 1. They do not recognize its importance. Instead, they are concentrating on steps 2 and 3. They are generally opposed to step 1 even though the evidence shows that it is imperative. Otherwise, the savings from steps 2 and 3 can always be negated by an increase in energy-dependent activity — as has been the case to date. Without step 1, there is no guarantee of the necessary savings. Recognition of this order of priority is, in our view, fundamental. Later chapters outline the means by which step 1 could be implemented fairly and effectively through changes in personal energy consumption and contain details of how this can be done.

THE GOVERNMENT

In recent years, a near-global scientific consensus on climate change has been achieved, consolidated by new research evidence. However, despite enormous pressure from members of both major political parties, the federal government has not enacted any legislation to reduce greenhouse gas emissions. Instead, it put out a broad policy statement in 2002 stating that it would adopt a strategy to reduce the greenhouse gas intensity of the American economy — how much is emitted per unit of economic activity — by 18 percent by 2012. Greenhouse gas intensity has developed from measuring energy intensity — used traditionally by governments to track energy use in economies. A typical measurement of greenhouse gas or carbon intensity would be tons of carbon dioxide emitted per dollar of GDP.

While indicators of greenhouse gas intensity are useful, they mask several underlying structural components. For instance, carbon intensity may reduce without any changes in energy efficiency, but only because the economy is shifting broadly away from energy-intensive activities, such as the shift from manufacturing to services. While this may seem like a good thing in itself, we should remember that the manufacturing activity has not actually abated but simply shifted overseas: The overall global carbon burden has actually remained the same if not increased. A recent study focused on disaggregating efficiency improvements from other factors in energy intensity calculations for several wealthy countries from 1973–98. All the countries showed declines in energy intensity during this period because of a combination of structural changes (that is, changes in the economy from manufacturing toward services) and real improvements in energy efficiency. For the United States, the annual reduction in energy intensity during this period was about 2.1 percent, with 1.6 percent attributable to actual energy efficiency improvements. It is therefore disingenuous for the government to now claim that it will initiate a new "climate policy" with average annual improvements of 1.8 percent in carbon intensity (which will amount to a fairly similar improvement in terms of energy intensity). This is no different, if not actually a little worse, from what would have happened anyway (the "business-as-usual" trend). In fact, a policy based on carbon intensity allows growth in carbon emissions and cannot hope to deliver the reduction the U.S. originally agreed to under Kyoto negotiations (a 7 percent reduction from 1990 levels by 2010).

The somewhat more encouraging news is that many states (twenty-eight as of December 2005) and more than one hundred cities have developed initiatives of their own for reducing carbon emissions and are pursuing cost-effective ways of doing so. But, with the exception of California, whose programs are relatively ambitious and a continuation of energy efficiency policies begun several years ago, these climate change action plans are modest in ambition. They are short of the United States' original Kyoto target. And they have yet to be translated into laws and regulations, which is to say that some of the hardest political battles lie ahead. Many environmentalists hope that these state-level initiatives will have enough momentum to induce Congress to take a more coherent view of the situation and pass nationwide legislation. This has yet to happen.

In an indirect way, the federal government does support some initiatives that could "reduce the rate of growth" of greenhouse gas emissions, given their strong upward trend, if not reduce them overall. In part, these initiatives can be interpreted as forming part of a continuation of its earlier energy conservation policies that first emerged after the "oil shocks" of the 1970s. Some of these policies are more recent and reflect a political consensus — albeit a weak one — to reduce energy use after the attacks on the World Trade Center and the Pentagon in September 2001. It was then that people began to realize that the country was overdependent on oil imports, mainly from regions of the world where a massive U.S. military presence to "protect oil" was causing resentment and anger.

In the rest of this chapter, we review policies adopted by state and federal governments in the United States in different sectors to try to answer the following questions:

Will state-level initiatives and other energy policy programs around the country be sufficient to achieve significant reductions in fossil fuel use to demonstrate that the United States is contributing its fair share to tackling the energy and climate change problems?

Do they represent sufficient progress toward the imperative of achieving a far more demanding reduction of emissions in the medium term?

TRANSPORTATION

U.S. surface-transportation policy is determined largely at the state level, with the exception that the federal government sets air pollution and vehicle fuel economy standards and provides some funding for building highways and public transportation. Policy on aviation and shipping is controlled entirely at the federal level. This is a consequence of the federalist structure of government specified in the U.S. Constitution, which permits Washington's involvement in the affairs of the states only where "interstate commerce" is affected. (In fact, the most profound such intervention by the federal government in any sector was in the 1950s, when a vast interstate highway system was constructed, hugely accelerating the growth of automobile ownership as well as the sprawl of building development.)

Vehicle Manufacturing

Policy on vehicle manufacturing is an important component of transportation policy. Following a huge spike in world oil prices in 1973, the U.S. Congress enacted legislation in 1975 that required car manufacturers to make an annual improvement in the fuel economy of the vehicles sold. However, since the early 1980s, manufacturers have lobbied representatives so effectively that fuel economy standards have remained more or less stagnant ever since. Furthermore, a loophole identified in these standards provides exemptions to so-called light trucks (which include sports utility vehicles, vans, and pickup trucks). In recent years, sales of these vehicles have risen by leaps and bounds, aided by clever marketing strategies that highlight their size, power, and safety.

As a result of these developments, while the average fuel economy of newly acquired passenger vehicles has been getting worse, the number of miles driven per driver has grown significantly. The main factors that have contributed to this growth are an interaction of land-use planning patterns and individual behavior, including the rapid rise of suburbia, a meteoric increase in vehicle ownership way above saturation, and a growth in travel. This is described in detail later in this chapter.

ENVIRONMENTAL ISSUES

Energy use in transportation has also been influenced by policy on local air pollution, congestion, and road safety. In 1991, the passage of the Intermodal Surface Transportation Act (ISTEA) marked a major shift in the way federal transport funding was allocated to states. A new focus on planning alternative approaches required city and state officials to examine a range of options for dealing with air pollution and congestion. In 1998, ISTEA was reauthorized as the Transportation Equity Act for this twenty-first century (TEA-21). Up to one-fifth of all federal transportation funding to states is now earmarked for public transportation. Nevertheless, the current share of people using public transportation is dismally low. In fact, between 1990 and 2001, the overall share of public transportation fell from 2 percent of all trips to about 1.6 percent. ISTEA and TEA-21 did however set the stage for transferring substantial amounts of money into bicycle and pedestrian projects, as well as for a few innovative public transportation projects that helped cities like Portland, Oregon, become less car-dependent.

SPEED CONTROL

In 1974, Congress imposed a nationwide speed limit of 55 miles per hour, with the intention of reducing fuel consumption. Prior to the adoption of these limits, most states had limits of 70 mph (with some having limits as high as 75 mph and Montana and Wyoming having no maximum limit). In 1995, President Clinton signed into law a transportation bill that included a provision eliminating 55/65 mph speed limits as a prerequisite for federal highway funding. Senior officials from the government's own Environmental Protection Agency expressed their dismay with the change, indicating that greenhouse gas emissions would thereupon increase by 6 to 15 million metric tons of carbon equivalent per year, with no increase in vehicle miles traveled. Ultimately, though, oil producers did not like the federal 55 mph speed limit because it reduced petrol consumption, and Congress gave way to their pressure by abolishing it, allowing states to set their own limits. Given the strong political power of the oil lobby and groups like the Automobile Association of America, it seems unlikely that this national speed-limit legislation will be revoked in the near future.

ALTERNATIVE FUELS

Chapter 4 referred to the scope of alternative types of fuel for reducing carbon dioxide emissions. Of all the renewable sources of energy in the United States, biodiesel has been one of the more successful in the last fifteen years, with a total of 325 installations by 2005, producing the equivalent energy annually of 132 million barrels of oil. Partnerships have been encouraged with communities, landfill owners, utilities, power marketers, states, project developers, and nonprofit organizations to overcome barriers to further development of this process by helping with feasibility, financing, and marketing. Recent experiments have also been conducted with biogas from animal manure at a new facility in Kansas projected to produce the equivalent of more than two million barrels of oil per year.

The blending of ethanol with gasoline has increased considerably since 1990. In 2005, 14 percent of U.S. corn production was used in this way. However, it accounts for no more than one-twentieth of all renewable energy consumed (including electricity). Intense lobbying by corn producers has generated strong federal support and state incentives encouraging its use. A few states in the Midwest and California have adopted policies to this end, but at current levels of corn-ethanol use, the reductions in net greenhouse gas emissions relative to gasoline are small, accounting for no more than 2 percent of U.S. transportation fuel. A recent U.S. transportation bill requires all future diesel engines to be capable of using biodiesel. However, to date, there is no government initiative to promote the highly expensive change that would be required for its significant growth, as that would mean having to change the entire vehicle fleet to accommodate the new fuel. In his State of the Union address in January 2006, President Bush announced that he was going to promote ethanol to reduce the country's "addiction to oil." But the following week, the very agency that would have to implement this policy, the National Renewable Energy Laboratory, faced a ten-million-dollar budget cut and announced that it would have to lay off forty workers.

About the only policy that the federal

government is pursuing directly in the interest of reducing greenhouse gas emissions from transportation is to provide $1.2 billion over five years for the research, development, and demonstration of hydrogen and fuel cell technologies. Hydrogen-fueled vehicles, the government claims, will primarily reduce the country's dependence on oil imports. The hydrogen will have to be produced from other fuels, such as coal, natural gas, or renewable energy sources. However, for the reasons outlined in chapter 4, the government admits that this can form only part of a long-term strategy that cannot conceivably be realized for at least two or three decades. The federal government has also required and provided financial support for certain of its own vehicles, as well as ones operated by cities and state governments, to use alternative fuels, such as ethanol and electricity, under the Energy Policy Act. It also provides tax credits for hybrid vehicles whose fuel economy is at least 25 percent greater than that of an equivalent conventional vehicle.

California — The Exception?

The state of California has been a pioneer in regulating pollution from vehicles, starting nearly four decades ago. The U.S.

Congress determined in 1970 that transportation-related air pollution control fell within the domain of the interstate "commerce" clause of the Constitution when it enacted the Clean Air Act. But because California had already begun addressing its air pollution problems a few years earlier, and has continued to do so more aggressively than the proposed federal legislation, it was granted a waiver from the federal law. Since then, California has raced ahead, with some of the world's most ambitious regulations on local air pollutants from vehicles. Because California has a huge automobile market and economy, it has effectively made automobile manufacturers sell vehicles that meet special specifications in its state.

However, even the strictest controls on local air pollutants may have little or no bearing on fuel economy. Indeed, vehicles sold in California have long had the same average fuel economy as elsewhere in the United States. But in the 1990s, the state introduced a policy requiring that a small proportion of vehicles sold should have zero emissions. Although this was later revised to allow manufacturers substantial leeway, a significant number of hybrid-electric cars entered the California market to get partial credits for zero-emission vehicles. More recently, the state has introduced legislation to set greenhouse gas standards for vehicles starting in 2009, with the goal of reducing the per-mile emissions from new vehicles by 30 percent by 2016. There is, however, a big legal question mark hovering over this entire project, given the circumstances of the original federal exception granted to California. Indeed, automobile manufacturers have launched a major case against the state government, the outcome of which has yet to be determined.

The state has no policies on travel-demand management, however, and seems to treat the increase in personal-vehicle miles traveled as a "natural" phenomenon, with officials often benignly commenting on how "Californians love to drive."

RESIDENTIAL ENERGY

As far as residential energy use is concerned, the policy emphasis is also largely on technological changes spurred by regulation or information and education programs. Some subsidies, funded both by general taxation and by utility bills, are offered to improve home insulation and the efficiency of domestic energy-using equipment.

New Housing

The most important influences on new housing are building codes, which specify the energy-efficiency standard that a property must meet. The inclusion of energy-efficiency requirements in building codes began in the late 1970s and has become widespread since then. Because building codes are implemented by state and local authorities, they vary considerably across the country. Generally they control only the fabric of the dwelling and not the energy-using equipment within it.

Although the role of the building codes in raising standards is widely welcomed, there are two common and complementary concerns. The first is that the regulations are by no means sufficiently ambitious or widely enough adopted: In 2004, only twenty-six states had implemented the latest residential codes for new housing or their equivalent. The second is that there is poor quality control, with the result that the prescribed standards are not met in practice. Estimates suggest that only half the potential energy savings have actually been achieved due to the gap between what should have been built and what was actually built.

EXISTING HOUSING

The Alliance to Save Energy found that if the set of policies they put forward for improving the efficiency of buildings and the energy-using equipment within them were implemented, national building energy use could be cut by about 14 percent by 2020. However, there is no legislation for raising the standards of the existing housing stock in spite of the fact that much of it is poorly insulated and the equipment used in it is wasteful of energy. There is a limited program of intervention for low-income households, known as "low-income weatherization assistance." However, while 28 million households are in theory eligible for the program, there are funds for improving only just over 100,000 households each year. Because of its small scale, this program does not yet deliver much in the way of overall energy savings.

OTHER POLICIES

There are several other significant policies targeting energy efficiency in the residential sector. Utility-based financial incentive programs have been in operation since the early 1980s, offering a variety of options including rebates, low-interest loans, and direct installation programs, which are leading to an accelerated market penetration of energy-efficient lights and appliances. Federal minimum efficiency standards are also in place for many residential appliances, including refrigerators and freezers, clothes washers, water heaters, and central air conditioners. These standards are being raised at regular intervals. The Energy Star, a voluntary appliance-labeling program, was introduced in 1992 to educate consumers about the advantages of purchasing efficient appliances. It is run by the Environmental Protection Agency and uses endorsement labels to identify which new homes and appliances are the most efficient on the market. The program also applies to products for the commercial market and covers over forty different product categories. It is estimated to have made considerable energy savings through influencing choices made by manufacturers, retailers, and consumers.

BUSINESS AND PUBLIC SECTORS

While there are no federal carbon emission policies in the business and public sectors, the government has continued to approve policies to promote efficiency in industry and in commercial and institutional establishments. The emphasis is again on technological research and development (R&D), voluntary agreements, and appliance labeling. In addition, the Department of Energy's Easy Ways to Save Energy program has been effective in educating organizations as well as consumers about the advantages of purchasing efficient appliances. It also works with state and local agencies to improve building codes and minimum efficiency equipment standards for commercial and residential appliances, such as air conditioners, furnaces, motors, and transformers.

Some states, notably New York and California, have made impressive strides in energy efficiency and renewable energy programs. These are reflected in effective policy interventions and efficiency programs that have led to reduced energy demand. By 2020, a saving of about 15 percent of their otherwise planned electricity generation is predicted. Cogeneration, or combined heat and power (CHP), has also shown a steady increase around the country. Depending on where it is used, a CHP system can as much as double the efficiency in applications that require both heat and power. It is one of the brighter spots with respect to energy-efficiency programs in the United States, although much more could be done. Currently, approximately 56,000 megawatts

(MW) of CHP electric generation is in operation in the United States, up from less than 10,000 MW in 1980. The government, in partnership with industry, has set the ambitious goal of doubling CHP capacity between 1999 and 2010. If this is achieved, CHP would represent about 14 percent of U.S. 2010 electric generating capacity. Other countries are, however, doing more: Denmark and the Netherlands get more than 40 percent of their electricity from CHP systems. The American Council for an Energy Efficient Economy estimates that a further 95,000 MW of CHP capacity could be added between 2010 and 2020.

Overall, industry is the only sector in which energy use and carbon dioxide emissions have not increased during the past decade. However, part of the reason for this otherwise commendable outcome is that it stems from a broad shift away from domestic manufacturing toward less energy-intensive service-related sectors. Increasing world trade has led to a transfer of some of the industrial base to countries where labor is far cheaper, so goods can be produced for subsequent sale in the United States at lower prices than was the case in the past. The consequence of this is that energy use in the United States industrial sector has fallen, as it has in other affluent countries. This then gives a false impression of success in lowering the country's energy requirements. Instead, what has happened is that the energy use of the countries from which the manufactured goods are now imported into the United States has risen in line with the transfer of the manufacturing base.

RENEWABLE ENERGY

While there is no comprehensive policy on renewable energy, there are a number of initiatives promoting it at the federal and state levels. The federal government, for instance, provides tax credits to individuals and businesses for the purchase of certain types of equipment that use renewable energy as well as, in some instances, grants and loans. It also has a major expansion of public funding to encourage more production of biofuels. Several state, and local governments and utilities offer similar packages of tax incentives and rebates especially for the purchase of solar energy equipment. In addition, "net-metering" permits owners of small renewable-energy equipment to sell excess electricity to the grid.

Some states have introduced Renewable Portfolio Standards (RPS) programs intended to require the utilities to generate a proportion of their electricity from renewable sources. Eligible sources include biomass, solar thermal, photovoltaics, wind, geothermal, fuel cells using renewable fuels, small hydropower of 30 megawatts or less, digester gas, landfill gas, ocean wave, ocean thermal, and tidal current. The most promising of these programs are in New York and California. New York requires suppliers of electricity to provide as much as 24 percent of their energy from renewable sources by 2013. California requires 20 percent by 2010, with the goal of reaching 33 percent by 2020. Most states have an RPS requirement to deliver 10 percent of their electricity from renewables by 2012.

Another state-level set of programs to promote renewable energy is the Public Benefit Fund. These are typically developed through the electric utility restructuring process to assure the utilities of continued support for developing renewable energy resources, for energy-efficiency initiatives, and for low-income support programs. Such funds are also frequently referred to as a System Benefits Charge (SBC) and are most commonly supported through a charge to all customers on electricity consumption, typically 0.2 cents per kWh. Some fifteen states have such funds, and, again, California is in the vanguard in terms of the amount of money collected and used to provide incentives for renewable energy producers and for consumer education on this front.

Whether California or any other state can meet more ambitious targets for renewable energy remains to be seen. For instance, although wind energy is seen as the leading candidate, especially for RPS programs, there is often opposition to developing huge wind farms for local environmental and other reasons detailed in chapter 4, and there is the issue of land availability in many states.

REGIONAL CARBON TRADING SCHEMES

In 2004, the governors of nine states in the northeastern United States agreed to form a trading regime to implement a "cap-and-trade" system for reducing greenhouse gases from power plants. The details of the scheme, called the Regional Greenhouse Gas Initiative (RGGI), were finalized in late 2005. A starting date of 2009 is planned and a target of a 10 percent reduction in emissions set for the following six years. There has been some discussion of similar initiatives in the western U.S. states. Within the RGGI region, however, both the power industry and some states are already talking about watering down these requirements, implying that either the political hurdles are too high or the justification for the initiative is not acceptable. Two states have already dropped out of the plan, limiting the region of the cap-and-trade initiative to only seven states.

COAL AND NUCLEAR ENERGY

In a bizarre twist of fortunes, recent rises in oil and natural gas prices, combined with an understandable concern about supply (the United States has less than 2 percent of global reserves of oil but currently uses 25 percent of the world total produced each year) have generated renewed interest in the coal and nuclear energy industry. About half of electricity production in the United States already comes from coal. Owing to the higher environmental costs of coal, it has been assumed for many years that natural gas would be the dominant fuel of choice in the future. Instead, numerous new coal-powered plants are currently being planned around the country, estimated to add tens of thousands of megawatts of electricity-generating capacity over the next decade.

In addition, "clean coal" is a new slogan that the federal government has touted as a means of keeping the country's energy supply secure: Two billion dollars are being spent on research and development of a new generation of energy processes that sharply reduce air emissions and other pollutants compared to older coal-fired systems (but not including greenhouse gases). Carbon sequestration research is also under way but, as outlined in chapter 4, its safety, reliability, and delivery at acceptable prices is by no means assured. No doubt for these reasons, none of the proposed new electricity generation coal-fired plants is planned to incorporate carbon capture and storage.

Meanwhile, government and the nuclear-industry advocates are calling for a new review of the case for a revived program of power station construction, though the findings of a review would appear to have been overtaken by decisions. In 2005, President Bush stated, "It's time to start building nuclear plants again," and Congress has offered substantial incentives to the industry in the form of a two-billion-dollar subsidy for a new generation of reactors.

Nuclear power accounts for about one-fifth of electricity generation in the United States. Recently, thirty reactors received twenty-year extensions on their expiring licenses and another forty are likely to get such extensions in the next few years. Several bills in Congress to put limits on carbon emissions at the federal level have provisions that would offer government loan guarantees for the construction of new nuclear power plants. Although promoted as a carbon-free option, serious doubts have been raised about the validity of this claim when seen in net life-cycle terms. This was noted in chapter 4, as were the concerns about nuclear power generation on grounds of proliferation, waste disposal, costs, and safety.

MISSING AND CONTRADICTORY POLICIES

What the federal and state governments are *not* doing, even with respect to energy policy, is at least as important as what they *are* doing. The most striking and important area that they have not tackled is air travel (the significance of which was discussed in chapter 2). There are also contradictory policies where priority is given to increasing road transportation despite the goal of decreasing emissions by improving the fuel efficiency of vehicles. There are policies with unintended consequences, and areas of policy where one government initiative is canceling out another. This section picks out some key examples and shows how even the best intentioned state-level "climate change strategies" are being undermined by policies in other areas for which governments have responsibility.

IGNORING THE INFLUENCE OF LAND USE

Land-use policy in the United States is determined by state and local authorities. It has been very much market-driven. It was set in the first half of the twentieth century by the Federal Housing Administration, whose mission was to promote home ownership, and explicitly directed to encouraging what was later called the "white flight" from many American cities into the suburbs. In effect, developers were encouraged to build houses on large tracts of land at low densities. The same policies were adopted by several states, predominantly in the West, which were still in the relatively early stages of urbanization. The associated sprawl was promoted historically by the construction of the interstate highway system and the proliferation of car ownership. The process fitted in with the federal government's lending policies on household mortgages.

Until the early 1960s, people moving to suburban counties received loan levels that were ten times higher than for those remaining in urban counties. The racial and economic segregation of American society that this perpetrated was expressed in a settlement pattern of largely white and wealthy suburbs contrasting with economically depressed black inner cities. Mortgage-lending policies today are arguably no longer racist, but a pattern of discrimination in favor of directing resources to suburbs and new development persists. Inner cities tend to be dominated by low-income blacks and other minorities, who typically live in rental properties because they cannot afford to own their homes. Meanwhile, although suburbanization caused enormous fiscal strains to pay for new public facilities such as schools, roads, sewers, and water supply systems, governments tended to subsidize these in numerous ways and often at the expense of the existing urban infrastructure.

The trend became so popular, however, that, throughout the latter part of the twentieth century, several thousand new housing subdivisions some miles outside the boundaries of main cities were incorporated. These suburbs and "exurbs" were almost entirely car-dependent in their design, and the provision of regular public transportation services proved too expensive, largely because of low demand for them. And the consequent growing sprawl has accelerated the vicious cycle of increased dependence on the automobile. What started out as a well-intentioned government policy to provide reasonably priced housing for the majority of citizens has since been exploited by developers and builders to sell the American Dream — a suburban house on a cul-de-sac with a two-car garage. However, as these settlements are miles away from shops, schools, recreation, and businesses, their inhabitants have become accustomed, or socialized, to spending a disproportionate amount of their time in automobiles. At the same time, a multibillion-dollar advertising industry has fueled their expectations of the car as essential to convenient living for over half a century.

THE RELENTLESS SUPPORT FOR AUTOMOBILITY

For more than fifty years, the United States has given automobiles and their drivers astonishing levels of support, far beyond what one finds anywhere else in the world. In many parts of the country, urban spaces have been "automobilized" — that is, designed to permit physical access to services and jobs only by car. For instance, in very many so-called urban areas of the country, it is virtually impossible to walk or even take a bus to a grocery store, pharmacy, or baseball game. Pedestrian access to many places is often abruptly blocked by enormous highway intersections or a sudden end to a sidewalk, with fast-moving traffic foiling any attempt to get to the other side. Stores are often built with huge open parking lots in front of them, so that a pedestrian or bus user would have to spend significant time to get to the shopping area from the road — not to mention the deterrent effect of carrying the goods purchased over longer distances. In addition, sprawl has also meant that public transportation services are infrequent and ineffective and, by and large, are used only by those who do not have cars.

In the past few years, politicians and other government officials have started to acknowledge, to varying degrees, the multiple problems posed by sprawl, including pollution, congestion, road casualties, loss of community life, and increased incidence of childhood obesity and poor health in suburbs. But that has not caused any state or the federal government to put restrictions on two of the main contributors to sprawl — automobile ownership and low density housing development. On the contrary, they have encouraged both through subsidies and low tax policies. The average number of cars per household has increased continuously throughout the last one hundred years. There are now nearly 1.2 vehicles per licensed driver in the United States, reflecting an absurd situation in which about one-fifth of all households have more cars than people! Average fuel taxes, adjusted for inflation, have stayed virtually constant over the past decade and, at less than a third of the retail price of gasoline, are lower than they were in the early 1960s and 1970s. In comparison, gasoline taxes in many countries in Europe are five to eight times as high as in the United States.

Over $10 billion per year is spent on marketing in the United States to sell about $300 billion worth of cars and light trucks. Taxes on the purchase price of vehicles are mostly set at the sales tax rates of different states, varying from zero to about 8 percent. But the bulk of the revenue is earmarked for the construction of highways and parking lots — less than 20 percent goes to support mass transit. Indeed, about 60 percent of funding for highways comes directly from fuel and vehicle taxes, thus maintaining the system of automobility as a well-oiled machine. Environmentalists have tried in vain to introduce so-called fee-bate legislation in several states to help develop some system of rewards and penalties for vehicles according to their weight and fuel economy at the point of purchase. Equally unsuccessful have been attempts to regulate sales of light trucks (whose market share has been beating cars in recent years) or to set other rules relating to fuel economy on vehicle purchases.

Even the most progressive states in terms of their climate change policies are quite backward when it comes to developing policies to curb the use of cars. California, which is in the vanguard of policy in the United States on climate change, is seriously wanting when it comes to regulating car use and sprawl. If the rest of the country has promoted car-based lifestyles, California has taken that to an entirely unprecedented level. Indeed, as one city planner observed as early as the 1930s, in California the car is virtually an extension of one's body, a prosthetic that is essential for providing people basic access to their jobs and services.

Very little has changed in recent decades. California's emissions control policies, as noted earlier, are geared only to reduce emissions per mile, not total miles traveled. Meanwhile, some 50,000 rural acres continue to be converted to roads and suburban developments each year. The state has a new strategic plan called Go California, whose very name evokes the image of more cars traveling longer distances and, perhaps temporarily, faster than before as a result of the construction of more roads and highways. While some money will be set aside for so-called Smart Growth initiatives in which new developments will be designed to be less car-dependent through mixed-use zoning, and for public transportation projects, this will be pitiful in comparison with the billions of dollars allocated for expenditure on highways.

OPTIMISM ABOUT HYDROGEN

In order to tackle the issues of oil security and climate change simultaneously, the federal government as well as the state of California have generated a great deal of publicity about their research and demonstration programs to aid the move toward a hydrogen economy. Some two billion dollars of federal money and tens of millions of dollars of state funding are being set aside for these programs. There is a bigger problem than technology at stake: It involves the complex issue of converting the massive fueling infrastructure in all parts of the country as well as a fleet of more than a hundred million new vehicles to be run on hydrogen. That involves lining up many ducks in a row, some of which are still not even in sight! Contrary to popular expectations, as noted in the chapter 4, the notion that hydrogen will be the climate change savior is far-fetched. Even by the governments' own reckoning, the first hydrogen cars won't be commercially available before 2015, and a fully operational hydrogen-based-car future will take at least another fifteen to twenty years beyond that to materialize.

Furthermore, if the federal government were really serious about promoting such a future, it would also have to pay close attention to the efficient production and use of energy in general, as hydrogen is not a primary source of energy but an energy carrier, like electricity. The transition will be much less expensive if much of the existing energy infrastructure could be freed up for making hydrogen. This requires electricity and natural-gas demand to be steadily and substantially lowered by reducing energy-dependent activity and widely adopting energy-efficiency measures so that, for instance, the cost of making hydrogen from these sources would be likely to fall. But the government has been stubbornly opposed to developing such regulations.

AIR TRAVEL AS A "BLIND SPOT"

One of the most important "missing" policies of government concerns air travel. As shown in chapter 2, air travel is the fastest growth area of energy demand. It currently contributes around 42 MtC to U.S. carbon dioxide emissions, and its contribution to global warming is between two and three times this, owing to the greater impact of the release of this and other greenhouse gas emissions at high levels in the atmosphere. However, the government seems unwilling to challenge in the rapidly rising demand for air travel. It is talked of in glowing terms as essential for growth and good for the economy. And not only is air travel not discouraged, it is actually strongly promoted through the provision of subsidies.

Funding for airport expansion comes largely from the federal government in the form of the Airport Improvement Program (AIP) and tax-exempt bonds. These amount to billions of dollars each year. The government also established an Essential Air Service program that subsidizes air services to over one hundred small cities in the United States. Meanwhile, airlines have steadfastly and successfully opposed legislation for a government-funded high-speed rail system that could be used to connect cities within five hundred miles of each other and thus provide a realistic alternative for many short-haul air trips. What is most disturbing is that nowhere in the policy arena — not even in the state climate change action plans — does air travel play a prominent role. The states keep assuming that the federal government will eventually regulate it, if and when it joins international negotiations on developing a firm policy on climate change. On the other hand, the federal government is not even focused on air travel from an energy and fuel perspective, let alone from a climate change one.

SUBSIDIZING ENERGY USE

Energy use is subsidized in many ways. The subsidies can be direct or indirect in the form of grants and loans offered at preferential rates. There are many federal programs that directly affect the energy industry and for which the government provides a direct financial benefit. The bulk of these subsidies goes to the fossil fuel sector (amounting to some five billion dollars a year) in the form of write-offs for exploration expenses, special tax benefits, export-import bank guarantees, and R&D expenditure. In power generation, the nuclear industry gets the lion's share of benefits, comprising 60 to 90 percent of the generation costs of power plants. Subsidies to the airline industry, mainly in the form of airport expansion programs, have already been noted.

Federal grants to states for public transportation have been skewed by states and municipal authorities toward rail projects rather than toward the far more cost-effective buses. These grants essentially subsidize rail travel by wealthy suburban residents into urban downtown areas (who are "choice riders" because they also own cars) instead of helping the poor improve their access to shopping and jobs within cities ("transit dependents"). While the new rail projects are generating more work-related trips by train in some urban areas, they are not encouraging transfer away from car travel of significant numbers of people who still rely on the automobile for leisure and social trips.

Perhaps more important than the direct subsidies paid to make energy cheaper at the point of use is the fact that consumers do not pay its full costs. Research shows that energy use creates external costs — that is, costs to the environment, not to mention costs to society — that are not covered in the price. In the case of transportation, these arise from traffic collisions, damage to local air quality, noise, and, of course, release of greenhouse gases.

Estimates of the true costs of transportation vary. In any case, there are many moral and practical concerns about determining monetary values for the future damage of climate change, making such estimates questionable. However, one study has suggested that transportation users are paying only about 20 to 30 percent of these true costs. By not requiring environmental costs to be borne by the user, by relentless support for automobility, and in combination with subsidies to encourage use of public transportation, the outcome is that *motorized* travel is effectively promoted just at a time when local, nonmotorized zero-emission patterns of activity need to be encouraged.

Keeping Us in the Dark

Without the right information, consumers cannot make sensible choices to save energy, either through purchasing equipment that uses less energy or is more efficient or by making behavioral changes. There is some information available to support purchasing more efficient equipment but little that focuses on choosing the lowest energy-using option. Similarly, there is almost no ongoing feedback and advice to consumers on how to operate their homes and cars in a low-energy way.

For household equipment, there are two types of information on efficiency and energy consumption available at the point of purchase: Energy Star labels and EnergyGuide labels. Energy Star is an award given for the best products in a category, whereas EnergyGuide gives comparative energy-consumption advice on all products available for purchase. As mentioned in the appendix, there are also a number of Web sites that list the most efficient household equipment and vehicles on the market. In addition, there is a Web site that enables people to find out how electricity sold by their company translates into carbon emissions. While these Web resources are to be welcomed, they are likely to be sought out by only a minority of consumers.

The Alliance to Save Energy advises that the existing information tools could be much more effective if the design of the EnergyGuide labels was improved, if only the very best products received the Energy Star awards, and if its standards were regularly updated, and if more funding were available for its work. Also there is no labeling system of any sort for old and existing houses and only a very limited scheme for new houses. This represents a huge gap in information, leaving consumers with no way of taking into account the energy characteristics of a home when buying or renting.

Similarly, the information offered to householders on their energy bills is hopelessly inadequate. Bills are often estimated rather than based on actual meter readings; they are not received until months after consumption; and they offer no specific information to the customer about the role of each component in the overall bill and how it could be reduced. There have been few innovations in the provision of information and advice to householders. This is a valuable but missed opportunity. Research has shown that good feedback or information enabling comparisons to be made between subsequent billing periods, or against the same period of the preceding year, or with the national average, can itself lead to significant reductions in energy demand that are maintained over time. No further interventions are required. The energy industry has shown little interest in providing this valuable information. Government could require it to do so.

In transportation, too, opportunities are being missed. Although new cars now have to display energy-use labels at the point of sale, even the most fuel-efficient cars with the lowest levels of carbon dioxide emissions are churning out more emissions than they were tested for because fuel-consumption measurements on new cars do not mimic the "real world" speeds and operations of cars. In fact, the actual fuel economy of vehicles can be as much as 30 percent lower than the information on the labels.

In an era of supposed consumer choice, the data needed to make informed choices that take the environment into account are often missing or incomplete. Labeled products do not necessarily provide the most relevant or even accurate information. The information is not supplied in an easily understood format (research shows that EnergyGuide labels are hard to understand) or in a timely fashion (e.g., energy bills). There are many opportunities to provide more comprehensive and comprehensible information to consumers at the right time —

without which making low-energy (and low-carbon) decisions will be impossible.

The Hidden Issue: Economic Growth and Energy

Wherever government policy is contradictory or missing, we are seeing increased energy-based activities. Most material prosperity is grounded in the use of finite resources: As we have become richer, we have acquired more possessions and adopted lifestyles that are generally much more energy-intensive than in the past. The government believes that technological development can enable this process to continue without increases in carbon dioxide emissions (or at least without increases in emissions per dollar of GDP). Chapter 4 reviewed the evidence for this view and found it wanting. Any optimism that technology alone can achieve the considerable carbon savings that are needed can only reflect wishful thinking rather than the outcome of reliable calculations made by a responsible government.

Proponents of the potential for the decoupling of fossil fuel use from production point to the fact that, over time, developed economies have tended to use less energy for each unit of GDP. U.S. government figures show that between 1990 and 2003, the economy expanded by 46 percent, while final energy demand grew by only 16 percent. While superficially impressive, this is accounted for partly by the energy-intensive industries being exported to other countries: It is a pattern seen in all developed countries, as the economy relies increasingly on service-sector activities. The apparent improvement does not offer hope that, as part of some sort of natural progression, energy use and carbon emissions will actually start falling as the economy grows.

Although successive federal and state governments have had energy-efficiency policies for many years, and some have even pledged action on climate change, their more prominent objective continues to be to promote growth in the economy. This is seen as the only way of providing the public with improvements in quality of life and an extension of choice. Any downturn in the economy is seen as a serious cause for concern because it is assumed that only out of the wealth created from economic growth can the essential basic services of health, housing, education, and defense be provided. It would seem that the essential services of an ecologically balanced climate system provided by the planet are taken for granted.

There are essentially two options for those who are not convinced that high levels of economic growth, as it is currently measured, can be made compatible with reducing greenhouse gas emissions:

1. Continue to prioritize economic growth, and adapt to the consequences of climate change.
2. Prioritize policies aimed at a major reduction of greenhouse gases to minimize the risk of serious climate change, and adapt to the consequent new economic circumstances.

Supporters of the first option either directly argue or indirectly imply that rather than prevent further climate change, we can adapt to it. Adaptation measures include constructing higher seawalls, building more reservoirs, constructing buildings to withstand an increased intensity and frequency of storms, and providing more help to developing countries. Some economists who support this view argue that our well-being would be better served by high levels of economic growth so that the high costs of adaptation to climate change can be afforded. They consider this preferable to lower economic growth and a less damaged climate, arguing that the cost of preventing climate damage is greater than the cost of the damage itself. Given the climate risks outlined in chapter 1 and the analysis outlined in chapter 6, this is clearly nonsense, and dangerous nonsense at that. As a Danish energy expert has said, pointing out the limitations of economic analysis: "It may not be cost-effective to save the planet, but we should do it anyway."

The extreme version of this position is heard less often now as the risks of climate change have become clearer. However, it forms at least part of the thinking of all governments. At the heart of the matter lies the belief that rising material prosperity through economic growth is a nonnegotiable aspiration. President Bush has regularly repeated the mantra that "economic growth is the solution, not the problem"; "economic growth and environmental protection go hand-in-hand"; "the power of economic growth [can be tapped] to further protect our environment for generations that follow"; "economic growth is the key to environmental progress because it is growth that provides the resources for investment in clean technologies"; and that adhering to the Kyoto Protocol "would wreck the U.S.

economy."

As we have seen, these positions are looking more and more untenable, and option 2, above — minimizing the risk of climate change — looks like the only way forward. Instead of sacrificing the planet to save the economy, the answer must lie both in taking effective action to reduce emissions and in reconsidering the role of economic growth. A distinction between those elements of growth and technological development that are beneficial and those that are injurious to the future condition of the planet and its populations is essential. To this end, new measures of progress will have to replace that of economic growth. They will be focused on improving the quality of our lives. These challenges, to rethink the basis on which we measure national and personal success, and to find new opportunities to create truly sustainable wealth are immense.

This book does not have all the answers to what is the right balance to strike between the two objectives of achieving economic growth and maintaining a stable climate. However, it is very clear that any economic approach that endangers the future of the planet, as our current model is doing, is unacceptable, no matter how much wealth is generated.

Looked at in detail, the different elements of climate policies in the United States present a mixed picture. Policy approaches vary considerably among different sectors and states. A few of its components have a good track record and targets are likely to be met, notably the efficiency standards in California and New York, and some of the proposed renewable energy strategies. In transportation, the challenges remain immense and the responses feeble. California's approach is commendable only because it stands out against the inaction of other states. But even there, by regulating *per mile* emissions from vehicles and ignoring the increase in *miles driven,* the outcome may be an insignificant reduction in emissions, even presuming the policies deliver on their intentions. Desirable as the medley of state-level measures may be, they seem more symbolic than capable of making deep cuts in emissions. Some optimists might say that these first steps are important. However, climate change is too serious an issue to allow ourselves to be content with gestures unlikely to bring about sufficient reduction in carbon dioxide emissions.

Indeed, even the California government, with its seemingly bold programs, is not preparing its population for the future changes that will be required to prevent serious climate change. For example, most savings in transportation are expected from a technical-efficiency policy for cars independent of consumer choice or behavior. Although the proposed savings are welcome, unless the public is informed about the need to reduce emissions by adopting economical driving habits and, more particularly, by lowering their mileage considerably, the improvements will not have a lasting effect. Neither California nor any other state government is being sufficiently bold. There is no evidence that the path to the intended "more sustainable, lower-carbon economy" is being pursued to anything like the extent essential to prevent hazardous climate change.

Current energy policies in the United States are by no means comprehensive enough to put the country on a path to a low-carbon future. Perhaps most starkly, they are ineffectual in comparison with those of other developed countries that have explicit greenhouse gas reduction policies. They certainly do not lay the foundation for the radical changes necessary to meet the requirement of a considerable reduction in carbon emissions over the next few decades.

The federal government has steadfastly refused to adopt any policy framework aimed at reducing energy consumption per se, let alone ensuring that the country contributes its share of the "burden" of the climate change problem. Even the policies in individual states that are designed to promote energy efficiency and a switch to lower-carbon fuels are, in the main, mostly "business as usual." This is not a realistic strategy.

To summarize the main points of this chapter:

- The U.S. government is not committed to reducing greenhouse gas emissions, in contrast to other leading developed countries, and remains content to ignore the fact that they are growing at an alarming rate.
- It is probably too late for the United States to meet its Kyoto target, even if the federal government now reversed its policy.
- Current government policies are not leading toward the fundamental changes required for a sustainable, low-carbon economy.
- More seriously, many government policies (and subsidies) encourage the

development of a higher-energy society, precisely the opposite of what is needed. Policy on air travel allowing for its continuing expansion is a perfect illustration of this failure.

- State governments and the federal government are unrealistically optimistic about the role of technology in providing reductions in energy use and carbon emissions, and there are limits to the reductions that can be achieved solely by win-win strategies.

- Economic growth is simply a means of achieving human well-being — as is reducing carbon dioxide emissions. A major reassessment of the balance between the economy and climate protection must be struck. The climate and our future cannot be sacrificed to save the economy.

6

TURNING THE TANKER AROUND

INTERNATIONAL NEGOTIATIONS ON CLIMATE CHANGE

Chapter 5 highlighted the many incompatibilities and inconsistencies in the policies of the United States — as of other countries. Designing effective policies will mean making hard choices and overturning long-held views. But we have no choice. There is no time left for believing that technology will get us off the hook, as we saw in chapter 4. Nor should we indulge in environmental tokenism. Radical changes in government priorities, practices, and policies are required to prevent serious climate change, and we as voters have to press for and accept the changes needed.

So how has the international community responded to this agenda? This chapter sets down in some detail the history of negotiations aimed at achieving a global approach to the problem and the role of the U.S. administration in the process.

As early as 1957, a committee of the National Academy of Sciences produced the "First General Report on Climatology to the Chief of the Weather Bureau." This stated: "In consuming our fossil fuels at a prodigious rate, our civilization is conducting a grandiose scientific experiment." Several years later, following a month-long workshop at the Massachusetts Institute of Technology in 1970, and an international conference in Stockholm in 1971, global climate change suddenly became a significant policy concern. New data and calculations began to convince scientists that the world's climate might change far sooner and more drastically than had seemed possible only a decade earlier. In 1976, a congressional committee began the first ever hearings to address climate change. While no one advocated reductions in carbon dioxide emissions at the time, in late 1978, Congress passed the National Climate Act, which provided some modest research funds on climate change.

At the global level, the World Meteorological Organization was conducting a research program on climate change. But it was not until 1988 that it decided to join forces with the United Nations Environment Programme to establish the Intergovernmental Panel on Climate Change (IPCC). In 1990, on the basis of an elaborate, international peer-review driven scientific process, the IPCC finalized its First Assessment Report. This confirmed that human activities were affecting the climate. This IPCC report and the Second World Climate Conference held in the same year helped focus attention on climate change and on the need for international action.

Since then, the world's governments have steadily woken up to the threat of climate change, though their responses leave much to be desired. In 1992, the United Nations Framework Convention on Climate Change (UNFCCC) was created. Its objective is for the world to achieve stabilization of "greenhouse gas concentrations in the atmosphere at a level that would prevent dangerous human-induced interference with the climate system." The gases in question include methane, nitrous oxide and, in particular, carbon dioxide. However, the convention did not define what level of carbon dioxide concentrations in the atmosphere would be dangerous or set an upper limit. The UNFCCC took effect in March 1994. One hundred eighty-nine countries are now signatories (known as "parties") to the convention. These countries continue to adopt decisions, review progress, and consider further action through regular, usually annual, meetings of its Conference of the Parties (COP) — the highest decision-making body of the convention.

Meanwhile, a parallel approach, discussed in chapter 5, was being championed, mainly by a group of American economists. This was based on an attempt to measure the current costs of mitigating climate change against the future costs of environmental damage from climate change. It required a monetary value to be applied to such factors as population displacement and death of individuals, including those not yet born. The economists simply assumed that it was reasonable to use models to compare what were in fact incommensurable goods — economic growth and a range of environmental outcomes — by hiding the essential questions relating to value judgments behind a technical façade. They then came up with the finding that a "do-nothing" approach was reasonable simply because the benefits of economic growth would be greater than the costs of damage due to climate change. However, it soon transpired that their methodology was based on a formula in which the same economic value was given to one dead European as fifteen dead Indians. Not surprisingly, the idea that the lives of people in poorer countries should have a lower cash value than those in richer countries caused outrage, and the governments of several developing countries denounced it as the "economics of genocide." It was formally repudiated in the "policy-makers summaries" when the IPCC Second Assessment Report was subsequently published in 1995.

This report led two years later to the adoption of the Kyoto Protocol to the UNFCCC. In the report, there was a cautious announcement that "the balance of evidence suggests a discernible human influence on global climate." However, this conclusion was challenged by some, and their "skepticism" was particularly influential in the United States. Frederick Seitz, president emeritus of Rockefeller University and past president of the National Academy of Sciences, publicly denounced the report, saying, "I have never witnessed a more disturbing corruption of the peer-review process than the events that led to this IPCC report." Seitz also distributed a petition during the 1997 Byrd-Hagel vote (see below) attacking the impending ratification of the

Kyoto Protocol on the grounds that it would "ration the use of energy." He said, ". . . This treaty is based upon flawed ideas. Research data on climate change do not show that human use of hydrocarbons is harmful. To the contrary, there is good evidence that increased atmospheric carbon dioxide is environmentally helpful. . . . It is especially important for America to hear from its citizens who have the training necessary to evaluate the relevant data and offer sound advice." Other skeptics like Fred Singer specifically attacked the "balance of evidence" statement in the report, contending that this was being misinterpreted by policymakers to mean that a global warming catastrophe was imminent.

The majority of climate scientists, however, including those who were not involved in the IPCC process, refuted Seitz and Singer. However, the doubts raised by Seitz and Singer seem to have created public and political uncertainty about the validity of climate change science in the United States (whereas in Europe their analysis had little influence). Yet, the scientific evidence for climate change was accumulating over the years, and when the IPCC published its Third Assessment Report in 2001, it confidently stated, ". . . There is new and stronger evidence that most of the warming observed over the last 50 years is attributable to human activities." The report warned that a rise of average global temperatures by 2°C (3.6°F) over preindustrial levels is an important threshold beyond which damage to human health and the earth's ecosystems would be especially dangerous.

The UNFCCC

Since its formation, the UNFCCC has included a strong endorsement of both the equity principle and the precautionary principle as the bedrock of the action needed to stabilize carbon dioxide concentrations at a safe level. These are the underlying principles of this book. On the first of these, it says:

The Parties "should protect the climate system for the benefit of present and future generations of humankind, on the basis of equity" (Article 3.1). They note that "the largest share of historical and current global emissions of greenhouse gases has originated in developed countries and that per capita emissions in developing countries are still relatively low" (Preamble). They therefore conclude "that in accordance with their common but differentiated responsibilities and respective capabilities the developed country Parties must take the lead in combating climate change and the adverse effects thereof" (Article 3.1), while, "the share of global emissions originating in developing countries will grow to meet their social and development needs" (Article 3.3).

Its position on the precautionary principle is expressed as follows:

The Parties "should take precautionary measures to anticipate, prevent or minimize the causes of climate change and mitigate its adverse effects. Where there are threats of serious or irreversible damage, lack of full scientific certainty should not be used as a reason for postponing such measures" (Article 3.3).

Precaution means that it is necessary to take steps to avoid climate change even if uncertainties remain as to the extent of the dangers faced. And equity recognizes differentials: that national responsibilities for the accumulation of greenhouse gases in the atmosphere thus far are actually very different when added up over time. In essence, the UNFCCC recognizes that the industrial countries of the North, with 20 percent of the global population, are responsible for 80 percent of the rise in concentrations, and the newly industrializing countries of the South, with 80 percent of global population, are responsible for the other 20 percent of the rise. Because of the link between emissions and income, per capita emissions (or impact) and purchasing power (or income) can be used as a measure. This reveals significant differences between the populations of the two groups of countries, acknowledged in the text of the UNFCCC, of the order of 10–15:1.

THE BYRD-HAGEL RESOLUTION

In June 1997, months before a major meeting of the Conference of Parties the U.S. Senate passed by 95 votes to 0 the Byrd-Hagel Resolution. This stated that ". . . The U.S. should not be a signatory to any Protocol . . . unless [it] mandates new specific scheduled commitments to limit or reduce greenhouse gas emissions for Developing Country Parties . . ." Interestingly, the resolution was not a denial of the science of climate change as such, but rather a declaration that the United States would accept the logic of action on climate change provided that the right framework involving all countries could be found. The resolution makes it clear that the United States would not sign up to an international protocol that required developed countries alone to take action on climate change.

THE KYOTO PROTOCOL

In order to put the objective of the UN-FCCC into action, the Kyoto Protocol was created. It was designed to be the first legally binding treaty aimed at cutting emissions of the main greenhouse gases. More than 150 nations signed it in 1997. In 2001, however, the U.S. administration announced that it would not ratify — that is, adhere to — the terms of Kyoto, just around the time when the global scientific consensus on climate change was secured and new threats like abrupt climate change and regional problems began to be discovered. The Protocol "entered into force" in 2005 when Russia finally ratified it. Under its terms, the "Annex 1" developed countries committed themselves to a range of targets to reduce emissions during the twenty-year period between 1990, the base year, and 2010. (Strictly speaking, the reduction target applies to average emissions of the five years between 2008 and 2012, but this is simplified here to 2010.) At present, nonindustrialized countries do not have targets.

The net effect of the treaty, if targets are met, will be to reduce industrialized countries' emissions by 5 percent. Clearly, the Kyoto Protocol, such as it is, is at best a preamble rather than a substantial advance in climate policy: The protocol's scientific advisers, the IPCC, say it will delay the effects of climate change by, at most, ten years. The hope of the proponents of the Kyoto approach is for the agreement to be the first step in a series of future international treaties that will bring about sufficient reductions in greenhouse gas emissions to limit damage from climate change and achieve the ultimate goal of climate stabilization. In theory, by operating under the protocol, countries will learn how to reduce emissions at the lowest cost and will set up emissions-trading systems to help them to do so. If the rules are designed correctly, emissions trading should mean that countries with cheaper emissions-saving options will do more than their agreed share, and will then sell their "spare" emissions credits to countries where national reductions are more expensive. The process will lead to industrialized countries transferring funds and technologies to developing countries to help them find cost-effective ways of achieving lower emissions. If it works as planned, the Kyoto Protocol would make a transition to a "low carbon" world easier.

The strong American political opposition to the Kyoto treaty has been a major blow to the process. Not having the world's biggest polluter on board undermines the authority and effectiveness of the protocol. The current U.S. administration under George W. Bush has been especially audacious in its rejection of the scientific consensus on climate science and of past commitments of the United States to an international climate-policy regime. But it is important to remember that the Byrd-Hagel Resolution was put to a vote during President Clinton's administration. Given its overwhelming passage, Clinton decided not to submit the Kyoto Protocol for ratification in Congress even though his administration had signed it.

The reduction target the United States agreed to meet under Kyoto was a 7 percent reduction in greenhouse gas emissions between 1990 and 2010. However, given the growth in emissions since 1990, it would now be virtually impossible to meet this target — a target that was seen as achievable when it was negotiated in the 1990s. In

2003, emissions were already about 17 percent higher than 1990 levels, representing an annual growth rate of just over 1 percent. To meet its Kyoto target, therefore, U.S. emissions would have to reduce at an *annual* rate of over 5 percent for the remaining years. Because the Kyoto treaty allows trading in carbon, in reality the United States would not have to meet all the reductions nationally — it could pay other countries to make savings on its behalf. Nevertheless, even with trading, trying to meet the Kyoto target from where we are now would require radical and fundamentally different policies and changes in individual behavior. Whether the enormous energy system in the United States can be expected to effect such a turnaround — even if there were the commitment to do so — is debatable.

However, if this is not possible, then it must be accepted that an expanding economy and protection of the global environment from climate change are irreconcilable goals. Yet, such reconciliation lies at the heart of the radical "Blue Green Alliances" of labor, conservationists, and environmentalists determined to work together to develop a policy with this objective.

What is equally a cause for concern is that

many of the countries that have agreed to the Kyoto Protocol are not on course to achieve their targets. In the European Union (EU), the latest assessment is that ten of the fifteen member states are likely to miss them by a wide margin. Even those countries that were allowed significant increases in emissions under the EU burden-sharing arrangements, including Portugal, Spain, and the Republic of Ireland, look set to fail in their commitments. There is still just about time for the EU to meet its overall targets if strong action is taken, but at present this seems not to be a political priority. While modest emissions reductions will be achieved, the Kyoto treaty, in spite of its weak ambitions, seems unlikely to deliver even on its unambitious objectives.

The underlying reason for pushing the agreement through was supposed to be to lay the foundation for future treaties and more ambitious reductions, rather than to achieve the fairly minor reductions in greenhouse gas emissions on which it compromised. The most significant problems are, therefore, that the United States, as the largest carbon dioxide producer in the world, has not joined the treaty, and the majority of supposedly supportive countries are highly likely to miss their targets by a wide margin. Rather than be a symbol of the determination of the world to tackle climate change, it now appears as a symbol of precisely the opposite, of the short-term (perceived) economic interests of a few countries taking priority over the long-term future of the whole world.

PROGRESS BEYOND KYOTO

There is a clear and urgent need for a global agreement on climate change to succeed the Kyoto treaty. Is there any prospect that the United States will play a more positive part in future negotiations? Some comfort could be drawn from the fact that the political landscape in the United States has changed since 1997 — though not by all that much. Four reasons could be posited for this. First, there is a powerful and well-financed anti-climate policy lobby composed mainly of producers and marketers of energy-intensive goods and services. In light of changing public opinion toward climate change, the lobby has simply learned to change its tactics. These imply that, although their actions may indicate otherwise, even highly polluting industries can be deeply concerned about the environment and resource depletion.

Second, as noted in chapter 3, thanks to the successful efforts of lobbyists and so-called climate skeptics, the public is kept confused and misinformed about the urgency and magnitude of the climate change crisis. Third, Americans have been taught over the years to feel supremely confident about technological innovation somehow "riding to the rescue." This is the sort of optimism about technology that allows people to feel complacent because they are aware of the fact that the government is "doing something" in the field of hydrogen research, even while they continue to burn fossil fuels and consume goods and services at ever faster rates. Finally, the structure of the federal government, the two-party political system, and the strong role of the president weaken the ability of elected officials to develop coherent long-term priorities that relate to issues far beyond their terms of office.

Some of these factors can be redeemed by an informed and engaged citizenry. It is to the credit of environmental groups around the country that federal government policies affecting climate change are widely perceived to be out of step with the critical consequences, although these are being recognized by a growing majority of the

public. Many of these organizations, frequently supported by concerned scientists,
some even within national laboratories, have
helped bring some of the critical issues to
the fore. But it remains to be seen whether
the momentum of their efforts will be sufficient to bring about the drastic changes
needed in U.S. policies and public behavior
or whether the changes will be "too little
too late."

CONCLUSIONS

International negotiations on climate change
have been a long and involved process. The
clear statements of the moral basis for
climate agreements embodied in international treaties have not been matched by
clear actions to meet the commitments
agreed to by signatory countries. One of the
biggest disappointments of the Kyoto process has been America's decision not to be
involved. However, other countries, too, are
in danger of delivering less than they prom-
ised under Kyoto.

Ensuring that the United States is involved
in a post-Kyoto agreement is vital. There
are reasons to be concerned that the United
States is not yet ready to be an active
partner or leader in future efforts to secure
global agreement on climate change. How-

ever, there are also individuals and organizations that are working hard to change this position. The United States has also explained the basis on which it could be involved in future agreements. Chapter 7 sets out a positive framework for a global climate agreement in which the United States should be a key partner.

■ ■ ■ ■

PART III:
THE SOLUTION

■ ■ ■ ■

7

THE BLUEPRINT FOR SURVIVAL

CONTRACTION AND CONVERGENCE

The conclusions that can be drawn from parts I and II of this book are that we need to think beyond energy efficiency and renewable energy and toward concepts of sufficiency, of social and institutional reform, and of personal changes that incorporate *much* less energy and lead to *much* lower emissions of greenhouse gases. This chapter describes the only global solution that, in our view, is practicable, equitable, credible, and can be assured of success.

Global, national, and personal solutions are vital because the 80 percent reduction by 2030 target that the authors of this book consider both essential and realistic works only to limit climate change sufficiently if all countries of the world are also engaged in emissions control and have equivalent reduction targets. As chapter 6 showed, the United States has hitherto shuffled its feet on the climate problem, although this does not mean that it cannot take the lead in the future. But, equally vitally, people within the United States must be engaged in the project — the government cannot do it without its citizens' support. This means devising a national scheme to share out the country's allocation of carbon dioxide emissions. Both global and national approaches are suggested in this and the following chapter, based on political realism and principles of equity and effectiveness.

CLIMATE CHANGE: AN ETHICAL ISSUE

It is now essential that climate change is seen as an ethical issue complementing the fundamental one of survival. Intergenerational equity must be acknowledged to be at the heart of policy because, as carbon dioxide emissions accumulate in the atmosphere for hundreds of years, much harm has already been caused and our current emissions are accelerating the process. The principle underlying this approach is the same as the ideal of sustainable development, which was expressed in the Brundtland Report of 1987. Our common future, as "development which meets the needs of the present without compromising the ability of future generations to meet their own needs." Equity is key for practical reasons as well. Without equity, transparent in its application, there can be no realistic prospect of public acceptance or political agreement to introduce the measures needed. As it happens, the richest countries that have the greatest capacity to act are the ones that not only have been responsible for historically high levels of emissions but are also currently the most highly polluting. Thus, they are the ones who should and will have to make the greatest changes under an equal-rights framework. In the same way, poor countries, historically having generated a much smaller fraction of emissions, must be given commensurate "development space" to provide economic benefits for their people. Luckily, given advances in technology and the prospects for a broader cultural push toward making alternative lifestyle choices, we are virtually guaranteed that their development paths will not blindly follow the disastrous trajectories of their wealthy neighbors. Nevertheless, from an ethical standpoint of providing equal shares, it is essential that they be given corresponding opportunities to those of rich countries to bring their citizens toward prosperity.

WHAT IS CONTRACTION AND CONVERGENCE?

A global solution requires global agreement. It is widely acknowledged that the Kyoto Protocol, the first international agreement on greenhouse gas reduction, though intended to lead to a succession of treaties, will deliver only modest savings in global emissions even if its targets are met in full. Future treaties will need to involve all countries of the world, not just the developed countries currently committed to reductions under the protocol. This means agreeing on a framework for a global sharing of the finite capacity of the atmosphere to absorb greenhouse gases without serious damage to the climate.

A brilliant, imaginative, and simple means of reaching such an agreement on emission reductions has been put forward. Known as Contraction and Convergence (C&C), it was first proposed by the Global Commons Institute (GCI) in the early 1990s. Recognition of its unique qualities as a framework for combating climate change has grown at an astonishing rate since that date. It is thought by an increasingly influential number of national and international institutions to be the most promising basis for global negotiations.

C&C is founded on the fundamental principles that "safe" atmospheric concentrations of carbon dioxide must not be exceeded, and that global governance must be based on justice and fairness. However, this latter requirement has not been included for moral reasons alone; the GCI also claims that it would be essential for getting agreement from developing countries to take part in global emissions reduction. Its phrase "equity is survival" encapsulated the point that there can be no global security unless climate change is restricted to a manageable level, and this cannot be achieved without all countries of the world sharing this common objective.

C&C consists of:

- Contraction: an international agreement is reached on how much further the level of carbon dioxide can be allowed to rise before the changes in the climate it produces become totally unacceptable. Once this limit has been agreed upon, it is possible to work out the rate at which current global emissions must be cut back to ensure that it is not exceeded.
- Convergence: global convergence to

equal per capita shares of the agreed contraction is phased toward the contraction target by an agreed year.

C&C is a set of principles for reaching agreement. In fact, it simplifies climate negotiations in a remarkable way to just two questions. First, what is the maximum level of carbon dioxide that can be permitted in the atmosphere? Second, by what date should global per capita shares converge to that level? Using C&C does not entail a particular concentration of carbon dioxide emissions as the safe limit, nor does it set a timescale for reductions.

Determining the safe limit for greenhouse gas concentrations in the earth's atmosphere depends on the sensitivity of the earth's climate to greenhouse gases and the rate at which some of these gases get sequestered in sinks. As noted earlier, according to the Third Assessment Report of the IPCC, an average rise of global temperatures by 2°C (3.6°F) over preindustrial levels is an important threshold beyond which there would be damage to human health, and the earth's ecosystems would be especially dangerous. This requires keeping long-term concentrations of greenhouse gases within 400–450 ppm in carbon dioxide equivalent.

The GCI argues that C&C offers a realistic "framework" to replace the "guesswork" involved in the Kyoto Protocol. The targets in the Kyoto agreement are not based on any reliable understanding of the safe, or at least not-too-dangerous, limits of greenhouse gases in the atmosphere. Rather, the reductions agreed upon were determined by what was considered to be politically possible at the time of the negotiations between the thirty-seven countries involved. By contrast, C&C would use the best current scientific knowledge to set maximum levels of carbon dioxide emissions in the atmosphere, and hence maximum cumulative emissions. While the date of convergence would be subject to agreement, the principle of equal rights for all would remove the potentially endless negotiations that would otherwise occur, with each country making a case that its contribution to global reductions should be modified in light of its special circumstances.

Another critical element of the C&C proposal is that countries have the ability to trade carbon emissions rights. Countries unable to manage within their agreed upon allocations would, subject to verification and appropriate rules, be able to buy other countries' or regions' unused ones. The lifetime of the allocations would be restricted (to, say, five years) to discourage futures speculation and hoarding. Sales of unused allocations would be likely to generate purchasing power in vendor countries to fund their development in sustainable, zero-emission ways. Developed countries, with high carbon dioxide emissions, would gain a mechanism to mitigate the expensive, premature retirement of their carbon capital stock. They would also benefit from the export markets for renewable technologies that this restructuring would create. At the same time, the application of the C&C proposal would not only have the virtue of making a major contribution to shrinking the gap between rich and poor, both within and between countries, but would strongly encourage the adoption of types of energy with low carbon dioxide emissions.

What Would it Look Like?

The impact of C&C on the emissions allowances for people from different countries can be seen in the scenario illustrated below (figure 8), in which the limit on carbon dioxide in the atmosphere is set at 450 ppm and convergence is achieved by 2030.

The C&C graph shows how levels of carbon dioxide emissions related to fossil fuels have evolved over time for six blocks of countries: the United States; other OECD countries (which includes all the EU and other European countries, Australia, New Zealand, Japan, and Canada); the remaining countries of the former Soviet Union (FSU); India; China; and the rest of the world. Not surprisingly, most of the historic carbon dioxide emissions prior to 2000 are the responsibility of the developed world. After C&C is introduced, for instance in 2000 in this scenario, there is a period of adjustment up to 2030, by which date equal emissions rights have been achieved. The graph assumes that there is no trading between countries; in reality, the pattern of emissions might be rather different from this, with rich countries emitting more, having paid the poorer countries for the privilege of doing so.

The graph shows how per capita emissions of carbon dioxide would change under this C&C scenario. The highest-carbon-emitting countries have to make the largest contributions to the overall reduction in emissions, so the change per capita required is greatest for the United States, followed by the FSU countries and then the OECD countries (excluding the United States). Emissions from developing countries would be permit-

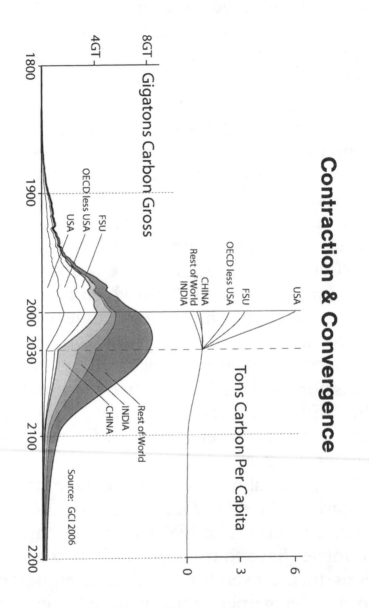

Figure 8: Carbon dioxide emissions under C&C (shown gross and per capita) for a maximum of 450 ppm atmospheric concentration achieved by 2100, with "permits" for per capita emissions converging to equality achieved by 2030. **Source: Global Commons Institute, 2006**

ted to increase until 2030. Thereafter, the emissions allowances for the developed countries would gradually reduce over time to ensure that the 450 ppm target was not breached.

FUTURE EMISSIONS UNDER CONTRACTION AND CONVERGENCE

As noted earlier, under C&C, the two key issues requiring agreement are the ceiling for atmospheric concentrations of carbon dioxide and the date by which international convergence is achieved. The effects of different choices on these crucial issues are illustrated below.

What is the level at which carbon dioxide should be stabilized? Scientists are increasingly of the view that the only way to avoid dangerous impacts is to limit global average temperatures to 2 degrees Celsius (3.6°F) above pre-industrial levels. There is continued debate about the earth's climate sensitivity, that is to say, the overall responsiveness of the climate to a doubling in pre-industrial greenhouse gas concentrations, which would tell us what 2 degrees Celsius translates into in terms of carbon dioxide concentrations. The prevailing consensus is that we may need to limit carbon dioxide concentrations to as low as 350 parts per million (ppm) if climate sensitivity is as high as many think it could be, or, if we're lucky, to 450 ppm. In what year can the contraction achieve these stabilization concentrations? Again, the consensus is that we must do so by the end of this century.

Figure 9 depicts this for two different pathways (450 ppm and 350 ppm). Although global concentrations of 350 ppm have already been exceeded, it might prove necessary to reduce concentrations back to this level. In the short term, concentrations would continue to rise, but as the figure shows, if global carbon emissions were reduced to very low levels by around 2050, then atmospheric concentrations could fall to 350 ppm by 2100. Not surprisingly, the remaining carbon budget, that is to say, the degree of freedom we would have to continue to emit greenhouse gases, is much lower in a 350 ppm scenario than in a 450 ppm one. Indeed, annual emissions may also have to be reduced much faster, very significantly by 2050 rather than by 2100, in order to achieve concentrations of 350 ppm.

The second issue to address is how quickly per capita emissions in countries of the developed and developing world should equalize, that is to say, how fast convergence

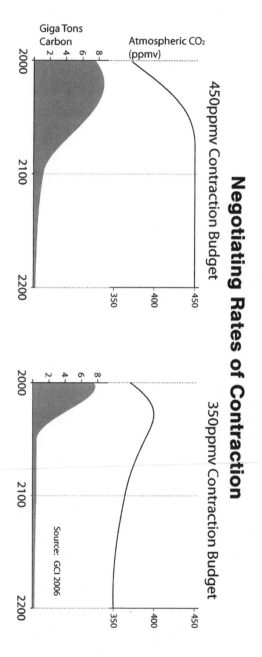

Figure 9: Emissions pathways associated with 450 ppmv and 350 ppmv stabilization concentrations. **Source: Global Commons Institute, 2006**

should take place. For a 450 ppm stabilization level, GCI suggests that convergence take place between the years 2020 and 2050, or around a third of the way into a one-hundred-year budget, for example, for convergence to complete. They also stress that negotiations for this at the UNFCCC should occur principally between regions of the world, leaving negotiations between countries primarily within their respective regions, such as the European Union, the Africa Union, the United States, and so on.

Figure 10 shows how the total carbon budgets and per capita emissions would work out for the developed world — the North — and the developing world — the South — for two different convergence dates. If convergence on a 450 ppm target was reached by 2020, people in the North would have to reduce their per capita emissions very quickly. The earlier convergence date would also mean that countries of the North would be entitled to a lower share of the global carbon budget than if a convergence date of 2050 were agreed.

How Could It Happen?

A framework based on C&C requires international agreement and political consensus. Although the Kyoto Protocol has turned out

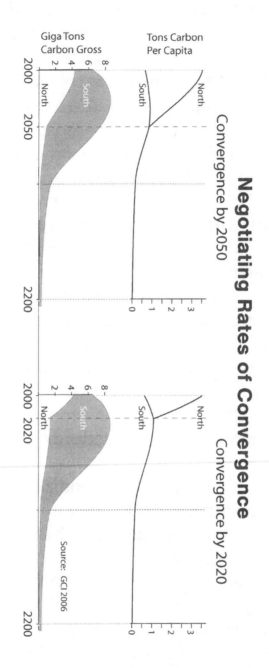

Figure 10: Two examples of convergence with a 450 ppm target. Source: Global Commons Institute, 2006

to be disappointing, there are good precedents for effective global action on environmental problems. One key example of this is the 1987 Montreal Protocol on reducing substances that deplete the ozone layer, which has been ratified by most countries. The other is the Convention on Long-range Transboundary Air Pollution — designed to abate airborne emissions that cause acid rain, eutrophication, and ground-level ozone — which is supported by forty-nine parties, including the EU. There is no doubt that climate change is a vastly more serious and difficult problem than either of these. Nevertheless, experience shows that, with the will to act, collaboration at the international level on critical environmental issues can succeed.

Recognition of the need for action on climate change should grow steadily as evidence of the damaging consequences of inaction accumulates. Over the years, commentators have suggested that disasters close to home will be necessary before countries act. Sadly, the WHO estimate of 160,000 people dying from global warming each year in developing countries, as cited in chapter 2, does not appear to have alerted world opinion to the need for urgent action. However, following the terrible impact of the 2005 hurricanes in the southern United States, no country can feel confident that it is immune to disasters that seem increasingly likely to be attributable to human-induced climate change. It seems likely that the increasing evidence of the effects of climate change is becoming harder to ignore.

As for the United States, it is clear that it will not come back to the table unless developing countries are included in a future climate regime. Beginning a clear and open debate about C&C is likely to demonstrate to the American public that C&C offers a logical and ethical approach to addressing the climate problem by ensuring collective responsibility. This may help clear the fog of despair among climate activists and others who seem locked into tired positions that are at least a decade old. It will also give Congress an excuse to revisit climate policy afresh, while remaining loyal to its original position articulated in the Byrd-Hagel Resolution.

Proposed Alternatives

In the course of several of the UNFCCC's Conference of the Parties (COPs), a small but extremely active group of policy analysts has emerged, each with his own approach to developing the global climate regime for the future. In a recent survey, forty-four distinctive proposals were discussed, including C&C. The alternatives vary in terms of their scope and style, with some seeking to extend the basic architecture of the Kyoto Protocol, others proposing policies and measures rather than quantitative emissions targets, and still others proposing a completely new framework. There are proposals that seek to include a subset of countries for negotiation rather than a global process, those that focus only on one or more aspects of negotiation, and ones that attempt to design an entirely new future climate regime.

While it is fruitless for our purposes to compare the entire range of proposals, it is useful to classify them into a few broad groups and to examine a few representative ones. But we should review only those that are relatively simple and unambiguous in their intent to address the climate crisis (as opposed to ones that avoid tackling emissions reductions on the grounds that it would not be "politically feasible"). Three such groups then become evident: burden-sharing based on historical responsibility; various market-based schemes; and so-called Kyoto-plus proposals.

The first is best characterized by the so-called Brazilian proposal, which was formulated and proposed by the Brazilian Ministry of Science and Technology in 1997 during the negotiations on the Kyoto Protocol. It rests on the principle that the responsibility of each country for inducing climate change be addressed not in terms of causes — that is, the greenhouse gas emissions — but in terms of effects, measured by the contribution of each country for the increase in the earth's surface mean temperature. The proposal is to set differentiated emission-reduction targets for countries according to the impact of their historic emissions on temperature rise.

Countries with a longer history of industrial development would bear a greater share of responsibility than those with shorter histories. Thus, with its greater share due to earlier industrialization, the United Kingdom would face a 63 percent reduction by 2010 against 1990 levels, while Japan's reduction would be less than 10 percent. This puts all the responsibility for emissions reduction on the older developed countries, excludes developing countries from quantified commitments, and has no formal concentration target. Therefore, the proposal contains an explicit escape clause for some developed countries, notably the United States, which argues that it will not be a signatory of any international agreement on climate change that does not involve a commitment from these other countries.

Market-based schemes typically try to reduce emissions by using some combination of carbon taxes and trading mechanisms. Some propose a carbon cap-and-trade system, in which a global emissions cap is established for each year and countries are allocated (or asked to purchase) "allowances," which they can then trade should they not be in a position to meet their respective "caps." Apart from their tenuous reliance on the market to solve the climate crisis, the main problem with these approaches is that they don't adopt an explicit framework of fair-burden sharing among countries to reduce greenhouse gas emissions. Without such an ethical notion to guide their strategy, it is likely that rich, powerful countries will negotiate their way to loose caps for themselves and find ways to exploit poor countries by "trading away" their own emissions allowances.

The third set of proposals refers to a variety of initiatives aiming to enhance the Kyoto Protocol's goals in a subsequent phase in which the world's largest emitters of carbon dioxide, as well as developing countries and countries with economies in transition, would join the international efforts to cut carbon dioxide emissions. Most of these initiatives recognize the need for developing country participation and some even have specific targets for atmospheric concentrations. The problem with most of them, however, is that they tend to be too cautious about stepping on "political mines" and therefore tend to be too complex and often fail to take a clear ethical position on addressing climate change.

Finally, there has also been some interest in building an equity-based regime that recognizes developing countries' desire for development, by allowing them to focus primarily on poverty alleviation rather than mitigation. The idea here is that even C&C may not go far enough in providing these countries a fair share of development space, given the relatively short time available for convergence. That is to say, by forcing developing countries to start their mitigation too soon, we may deprive them of a fair chance to address poverty and improve living standards sufficiently. There may, however, be some alternative ways to address this issue within a basic C&C framework by providing them with additional carbon credits in accordance with their share of cumulative historical emissions or by making explicit transfers to assist them with adaptation needs.

A review of proposals for tackling climate change published by a leading U.K. think-tank, the New Economics Foundation, concluded that the GCI's C&C strategy is the only one that offers assurance of, first, arriving at a defined atmospheric concentration; second, the equitable allocations that developing countries have rightly stated are an essential part of any agreement; and, third, the potential for immediate implementation.

THE U.S. POSITION

The United States has not made a formal statement regarding its attitude to C&C as a framework for future climate negotiations. However, U.S. policy statements have consistently insisted that if dangerous climate change is to be averted, a global response involving all nations is required. This was the principle outlined in the Byrd-Hagel Resolution, discussed in chapter 6. Given this view, C&C at least in theory, should prove attractive to the U.S. government. It too is based on the principle that all countries must be involved in the solution to climate change. Furthermore, it would create a global system of emissions rights which could then be traded between nations — allowing emissions reductions to be made at the lowest possible cost. This is another characteristic of C&C that fits with American statements about the sort of global climate change agreement they could sign up to. Furthermore, despite its unwillingness to take a lead on reducing emissions, as a signatory to the United Nations Framework Convention on Climate Change, the United States is committed to the stabilization of greenhouse gas emissions concentration in the global atmosphere — the objective of C&C. In summary, none of America's public positions on climate negotiations conflicts in any way with the basic C&C solution, namely achieving equal per capita tradable entitlements for everyone on the planet by an agreed date under a predefined global cap.

INTERNATIONAL SUPPORT FOR C&C

A large number of national and international bodies have endorsed C&C as the right way to tackle climate change and have published statements supporting it as the framework for negotiations. Since 1997, these have included key government spokesmen in China, India, and the Africa Group of Nations to the UN climate negotiations. It has been endorsed by most European environment ministers and by the overwhelming majority of MPs (elected representatives) in the European Parliament. The All-Party Parliamentary Climate Change Group of MPs in the United Kingdom is promoting C&C. Other organizations lending their support are as diverse as the worldwide membership of the United National Environment Program Financial Initiative, and two of the world's largest insurance companies. Numerous non-governmental organizations (NGOs) and academic institutions have also backed it, and the Intergovernmental Panel on Climate Change Third Policy Assessment has acknowledged its logic. The World Council of Churches and other religious organizations have called for a commitment to the framework, and the World Bank has published statements recommending C&C as the basis for effectively and equitably reducing greenhouse gas emissions.

CONCLUSIONS

This chapter has detailed the concept of Contraction and Convergence based on the principles of equity and survival on which it is founded. The proposal represents an international framework within which each country then makes its fair contribution to ensuring that a safe climate is maintained. In the judgment of its proponents, including the authors of this book, there is no realistic alternative. Once agreed, its success in reducing emissions is assured because the rates of contraction and convergence are set to that end.

Without doubt, there is an essential need both for public backing and for political leadership in climate negotiations to get all countries "on board." Moreover, all-party consensus is required, as the negotiations will continue to focus on international political agendas for decades, beyond the life of particular administrations. The international support that C&C has gained at political, institutional, and professional levels during the last ten years provides strong grounds for optimism about the prospects of its being "the only way to save the planet."

Chapters 8 and 9 detail how C&C can be implemented within each country by a system of personal carbon allowances allocated annually to its citizens.

8

FAIR SHARES FOR ALL

PERSONAL CARBON
ALLOWANCES

Within a global agreement to reduce carbon dioxide emissions, how is a reducing national allowance to be allocated? Our proposal is that carbon emissions from individuals' direct use of fossil fuels should be subject to a personal carbon allowance. The words *allowance, entitlement, quota,* or *ration* are alternative descriptions of the same concept originally proposed by Aubrey Meyer, founder and director of the Global Commons Institute and the principal author of this book. It was later developed by David Fleming, of the Lean Economy Institute, with the term *domestic tradable quotas* (DTQs) being coined, and is now the subject of detailed research by Kevin Anderson and Richard Starkey, of the Tyndall Centre for Climate Change Research. The main features of these allowances would be:

- Equal allowances for all individuals,

with only rare exceptions.

- Annual reduction of the allowance, signaled well in advance.
- All personal transportation and household energy use included.
- Allowances are tradable.

THE CARBON ALLOWANCE SYSTEM
EQUAL ALLOWANCES

Based on the same equity principle embodied in the Contraction and Convergence framework, it is proposed that everyone is given an equal carbon allowance — in effect, an equal "right of emissions." Some adjustment will be made for children because they add little to the energy requirements in their households. The system would need to be kept as simple and transparent as possible. Some exceptions may have to be made, and some individuals may get an additional allowance. However, these exceptions would be very limited, as the more that were granted, the lower would be the carbon allowance for the rest of the population. In general, people will be given incentives and helped to reduce their need for energy, to improve the efficiency with which they use it and to use, where possible, energy derived from renewable sources in order to live more easily within their carbon allowance.

REDUCING CARBON ALLOWANCES

Carbon allowances will have to decrease steadily every year in line with negotiated international reductions. The reductions may have to be revised at intervals, say every five years, in light of the latest scientific evidence on the level of concentrations of greenhouse gases in the atmosphere. Within each country, the carbon allowance will also have to be reviewed at intervals to take account of any rise or fall in the national population. By giving due warning of the annual reduction in the future allowance, people will be able to make changes to their homes, their transportation arrangements, and their general lifestyles at the least cost and in the way that suits them best. We believe that adaptation will be accommodated through the required learning process in the same way as many people in retirement adjust to a declining income. Improving carbon literacy, information, and advice will also help people to live within or below their allowances.

Personal Transportation and Household Energy Use

By including all personal transportation and household energy use in the allowance, a significant proportion of the energy-related emissions of carbon dioxide in the economy will be covered. What would not be covered is the contribution made by the business, industry, commerce, and public sectors, which produce the goods and services we all use. In due course, it may be possible to cover individual use of these by calculating the "embodied" emissions in, for example, producing, distributing, and retailing an apple, a television, or a car — and including these within a wider rationing system. However, this would be both complex and data-intensive as well as very difficult to apply to some goods and services: For instance, how could you "carbon rate" a hospital stay? Initially, therefore, we propose that the nonresidential sector be made directly responsible for reducing its share of carbon dioxide emissions, with a separate scheme envisaged for nonpersonal energy use (see below).

Tradable Allowances

Trading is a key feature of the system of personal carbon allowances. Indeed, the efficiency and effectiveness of the system will depend on people buying and selling allowances. Trading will ensure that carbon savings are made at the least cost to society, and that individuals have flexibility in adjusting to a lower carbon lifestyle.

The introduction of carbon allowances will bring in a self-reinforcing social and financial system that enables and rewards people for living within their rations. Those who have less energy-intensive lifestyles or who invest in energy efficiency and renewable energy may not use all of their annual allowance. They will therefore have surplus units to sell, thereby making a contribution to their income. Those who make many long journeys or who live in very large or inefficient homes will need to buy this surplus so that they can continue with something like their accustomed lifestyles.

Carbon allowances will create both winners and losers — people who have lower than average emissions and who thus have a surplus to sell, and those with higher emissions who would have to buy extra emissions rights if they wanted to maintain their patterns of energy use. From what we know about patterns of energy use across the population, it is clear that, at least in the early years of personal carbon rationing, well over half the population will be financially better off, as the allowance will be determined at the average level of carbon dioxide emissions.

The fact that there will be more winners than losers and that in general the losers will be the wealthier part of society who can better afford to buy spare rations (or preferably invest in efficiency/renewable energy) are clear political benefits. In order to communicate these benefits, it will be important to engage groups who will gain, such as lower-income householders and people who do not travel by air, so that their voices are heard strongly in debates about carbon rationing.

The price of a unit of the allowance therefore will be determined by the availability of the surplus set against the demand for it. In effect, a market will be created for carbon trading, possibly via a government clearing bank or a regulated eBay-type system. The phased reduction over the years will ease the transition toward sustainable patterns of activity. In addition, we foresee informal bartering taking place — for example, those who car-share might contribute to the carbon allowance as well as to the cost of the fuel. In effect, our proposal is based on what we have termed a new "conserver gains principle" to complement the conventional "polluter pays principle." Those whose lifestyles make a low impact on the environment are rewarded directly by those whose lifestyles make a high impact.

In effect, carbon allowances will act as a parallel currency to real money. People will learn to budget with carbon: They will be discouraged from using all their allowances before the end of the year and encouraged to be prudent in the same way as they are now with money.

ADMINISTRATION

Administering a system of carbon allowances should be simple. Each person would receive an electronic card containing the year's credits (see illustration below). This smart card would be presented every time energy or travel services are purchased, and the correct number of units would be deducted. The technologies and logistics would be no different from debit card systems. There is a manageable number of suppliers of household energy, transportation fuels, and air travel, and flows of fossil fuels are already very well recorded and tightly regulated in the economy. Introduction of the system would therefore affect only large companies that could easily apply it. To ensure that the introduction of carbon allowances would not be too complex, we suggest that initially the system should exclude journeys by public transportation, as these account for only low levels of emissions.

Carbon Allowance Card 2010

1234 5678 9101 1121

Valid from 1/10   Expires end 12/10

Ms A N Other

BEYOND THE INDIVIDUAL

One objection to personal carbon allowances is that it puts all the responsibility for reducing carbon dioxide emissions on individuals inspite of the fact that they have only limited power to act. Their emissions are determined by many factors — some of which are not in their power to change, such as the types of household energy or vehicles available and the mix of fuels used by their electricity supplier. However, we anticipate that technology and market forces will respond to rising public demand for help to prevent use of the annual allowance being exceeded in light of the expense of buying surplus units and to enable some to have a surplus, with a likely rising value annually to sell. The introduction of a number of social, technical, and policy innovations can be foreseen: The utilities could record their customers' carbon dioxide emissions on their energy bills, as electricity suppliers are being obliged to do under new legislation within the European Union. On the technical side, "smart meters" in the home could show people how much of their allowance for the year was left, which appliances were using the most energy, and how much carbon could be saved, for example, by heating bedrooms only in the late evening. In the future, new houses might have sophisticated carbon-management systems installed that made these decisions automatically and guaranteed that customers stayed within their limits.

In terms of policy, the system is highly likely to accelerate the take-up of new technology, the switch to utilities that supply electricity from renewable sources, appliances that are low carbon in manufacture and use, and so on. We believe that public pressure will prove far more effective in promoting "green" providers than by government regulating or subsidizing them directly through state subsidies or sales-tax breaks. The process will be furthered by official approval ratings shown on product labels, incorporating better information for instance, on electrical items about their usage of energy and consequent carbon emissions. It will be in the interest of manufacturers to supply low-energy goods because this is where the demand will lie. Socially, it could be expected that values would gradually change so that thrift rather than profligacy in energy use becomes increasingly valued.

LEARNING FROM EXPERIENCE

There has been no experience of long-term rationing — another way of describing the allowance — in the United States. The most familiar parallel is the food, gasoline, and clothing rationing introduced in many European countries at the beginning of World War II, when consumption of these commodities had to be reduced drastically as part of the war effort. For instance, in the United Kingdom, the food element of the personal ration covered a fixed quantity of meat, bacon, eggs, cheese, fats, sugar, and preserves. The principle of a flat-rate ration for all was justified because not all foodstuffs were subject to rationing. In addition, it was recognized that certain categories of the population had special nutritional requirements and therefore other schemes were superimposed on this common basis. For some items of food the system was maintained into the early 1950s.

Food rationing to some extent evokes images of hardship and therefore may be considered a negative exemplar for personal carbon allowances. But, rationing, coupled with subsidies and price controls, reflected and therefore promoted the concept of equity, in contrast to the intense inequalities that had existed previously. Despite difficulties, rationing was seen as fair, it was not seriously challenged, and opinion polls showed that it retained public support throughout the period of its imposition. An interesting aside is that overall nutrition and health also improved.

The need for carbon limitation is likely to be felt less immediately than the need for food rationing, which was introduced at relatively short notice. If society had not accepted rationing and, associated with that, price controls, many people would have gone hungry or even starved. Although a similar urgency applies to climate change, for most people it does not yet feel this way. While it will be more difficult to introduce, the concept of carbon allowances will in some respects be less prescriptive and intrusive in everyday life as compared with food rationing. People will be able to use their allowances as they please and adopt a wide range of lifestyle, behavioral, and technological changes to live within their allowances. Buying additional allowances will not be considered cheating, but an essential freedom within the system.

How Can This Happen?
Public Support

Only the government can introduce a system of personal carbon allowances that requires everyone to contribute his or her fair share in ensuring that the planet will not be handed over to the next generation in a deteriorating condition. But the government will require public support for the introduction of carbon allowances. Such support is vital, both in supporting and lobbying government for the introduction of personal carbon allowances, and in embracing the new system with a commitment to greatly limit those aspects of their lives that are energy-intensive. The alternative approach — of voluntary reductions in emissions by individuals requiring less intervention by government — could not even begin to tackle the scale of the problem because few individuals could be expected to start taking action for the common good, with "free riders" having so much to gain.

There has never been a greater need for organizations with very different agendas to work together to promote understanding of climate change as well as to communicate the necessity for personal involvement in reducing emissions. That may seem problematic. But public perceptions and organizational contributions could change rapidly as more politicians and influential individuals declare their positions on the issue and acknowledge that current policies and practices are dangerously unsustainable. Although the number of individuals who are active in calling for a sufficient response to climate change is very small at present, a domino effect can be foreseen. Some environmental campaigns have been effective, usually without any political affiliation, in striking a chord among the younger generation — those who will have to pay the higher price for this generation's dilatoriness.

POLITICAL CONSENSUS

As the damaging consequences of climate change become more and more evident, the adoption of carbon rationing and the need to curb the impacts of human activity that causes climate change will need to rise rapidly to the top of the political agenda. It would be devastating if there were no common purpose and instead political groupings vied with one another to obtain electoral support by making less demanding commitments on climate change in their manifestos. Short-term political decisions cannot be allowed to override the development of a common front that reflects the criticality of the issue of the future of the planet. Agreement between the Republican and Democratic parties therefore is very likely to prove essential. Given the absence of any effective alternative to rationing, we must hope for the development of a broad political consensus on this in the near future.

EDUCATION, INFORMATION, AND ADVICE

Education is essential to help impress on all levels of society the gravity of climate change and of the necessity for urgent action. As well as the political parties, industry, financial institutions, civil society, schools, and bodies with moral authority, including, of course, the churches and other faith groups, will have to be involved. Educators will need to work more closely with schools on environmental issues related to climate change so that they form a key element in citizenship classes where children learn the importance of sustainability, its relationship with their lifestyles and those of their parents, and its role in protecting the future integrity of the planet.

The media have a key role to play in this. They are the primary source of public information. However, as noted in chapter 3, a major problem lies in the conflict between their commercial self-interest and the wider public interest: A great deal of advertising revenue for television, newspapers, and other outlets is derived from cars, air travel, foreign-destination vacations, and other high-carbon products and services. Along with other business sectors, the media will have to adapt to contribute to a lower-carbon society. They cannot be relied upon to take a leadership role. Alternative routes for impartial information and advice and the options open for effective action by individuals need to be identified. Suggestions are put forward in chapter 9 on the form that this could take.

IF NOT THIS, THEN WHAT?

Are there any alternative policy options to personal carbon allowances for reducing carbon emissions? The usual policy instrument used to reduce consumption is price rises via taxation — and this is the key alternative to carbon allowances. As mentioned earlier, taxation of energy in the United States is at much lower levels than in European countries, so in theory there is much scope for raising taxes. Though seen as little different from traditional energy taxes under a new guise, several European nations have introduced a tax on carbon. However, the level of price increase required to deliver even Kyoto Protocol targets would have to be extremely high. In Europe, carbon taxation has been used as just one of many policy tools, and nowhere has taxation been high enough to drive down energy consumption sufficiently on its own.

Research from the United States shows just how high carbon taxation might have to be. Recent studies in the United States on fuel price elasticity, or the percentage change in fuel consumption caused by a 1 percent change in its price, have produced varied results. The middle range of these estimates is that a 10 percent fuel price increase is likely to reduce driving by no more than 1.5 percent in the short run and 3 percent over the long run. Thus, the taxation levels required to reduce consumption would be certain to run into very strong public opposition. There is a history in both Europe and the United States of resistance to increases in energy taxation.

There are a number of other problems associated with pricing as the route to curbing emissions. First, it does not have the same moral basis as rationing or the same psychological resonance. Because of the nature of taxation, it would not engender the same "all in it together" social cohesion toward the goal of lowering emissions as would rationing based on equal carbon shares. Second, reducing demand exclusively through raising prices is inherently regressive because lower-income households spend a greater proportion of their income on energy than do the better-off. Third, its effectiveness varies according to the trade cycle. A tax rate that achieves its objective in a period of strong economic growth may be much too harsh when that same economy is in recession. Finally, in contrast to raising prices, rationing has the advantage of certainty of result. The overall carbon savings can be predicted because this is precisely what determines the level of the carbon allowance.

WINNERS AND LOSERS

The implementation of a system of carbon allowances will have its losers as well as its winners, with significant effects on government and the business community as well as on individuals. For instance, as fossil fuel energy use declines, unless tax rates on energy rise, government will receive diminishing revenues from this source. On the other hand, less revenue will have to be raised to cover public expenditure on such items as road and air travel infrastructure. Moreover, consumer demand in spheres of the economy that are not energy-intensive, such as regional tourism, local shopping, and social and leisure activities, is likely to rise steadily. In addition, under a mandatory system of carbon allowances, many sectors of the economy will be increasingly motivated to prioritize their investment in favor of products and services with low carbon outputs. While of course major job losses can be expected in energy-intensive industries, this will be offset by job creation in industries that benefit from the adoption of the system.

Although this book has not specified a mechanism by which carbon allowances and reductions will be introduced for industry, commerce, and the public sectors, their scale of reduction will have to match that of the residential and personal transportation sectors. There may need to be a parallel system of rationing with a reducing allocation over time. Organizations would obtain or be allocated a carbon allowance, perhaps by tender — that is, a form of auction modeled on the issue of government debt. Initially, organizations are likely to be focused on increasing energy efficiency and moving away from fossil fuels. However, over time, the broader structure of economic activity is likely to shift in favor of services as demand for old, energy-intensive practices falls away.

Some of the possible winners and losers in an increasingly low-carbon society are listed in table 1 (see next page). It is clear that, under the system, there will be no shortage of new entrepreneurial opportunities for business and commerce.

It can be seen that many in the "losers" column, such as some manufacturing and construction companies, are also active in

Table 1: Business Winners and Losers Under a Low-Carbon Economy

Winners	Losers
Manufacturers of efficient low-energy appliances and vehicles	Manufacturers of energy-inefficient appliances and vehicles
Bus and bicycle manufacturers	Car manufacturers
Bicycle retailers and repair shops	Car showrooms, garages, and gas stations
Construction industry retrofitting existing buildings to make them more energy-efficient	Industry involved in transportation infrastructure construction
Businesses offering low-energy/carbon solutions, e.g. zero-energy homes	Businesses selling high-energy systems, e.g., air-conditioning in homes
New technologies such as micro CHP (combined heat and power), heat pumps, hybrid cars, and airships	Old technologies such as direct electric heating systems
Renewable energy producers, e.g., of wind turbines, solar water heating, and biofuels	Fossil fuel industries involved in the extraction, processing, and supply of fuel
Local food producers and organic farmers	Conventional energy-intensive agriculture
Local shops and businesses	Regional shopping centers
Domestic and regional tourism	Long distance and overseas tourism
International communication systems	Airlines

the "winners" column. For example, those currently involved in new transportation infrastructure projects are also involved in building schools and hospitals and in providing housing. Major energy companies also have considerable investment in the development of wind energy and solar power, and many appliance manufacturers produce both efficient and inefficient products. Those currently working on oil rigs may use their skills in the future on the construction of wind farms. Some of today's companies are already in a good position to adapt to a lower-carbon environment. Indeed, the history of the development of business and commerce shows that diversification has always been a key to sustained corporate success.

Industry is typically concerned about international competition. However, on the assumption that C&C is chosen for global agreement on greenhouse gases, all economies will be working within similar constraints and will be increasingly focused on progress toward a low-carbon future. Moreover, the earlier a company, or indeed a nation, takes steps toward reducing dependency on fossil fuels, the better position it will be in to sell low-carbon technologies and expertise abroad.

Over the years, the concept of C&C and carbon rationing has been presented by the authors to a wide range of both professional and general audiences. Not everyone is convinced that it is the right solution and many questions arise. These are often underpinned by one of two viewpoints. One is the belief that there must be a better means of achieving the necessary reduction in carbon dioxide emissions. But if it is not the right answer, then another equally effective solution is required. As noted in chapter 7, we have been unable to identify one. Alternatively, the questions reflect the dangerous view that current policy, based on advice and exhortation, and on developments in the field of technology, will enable us to muddle through as we have in the past. The assumption is that this laissez-faire approach will be able to deliver that reduction without the need to prescribe limits on personal choice.

Two issues raised frequently by audiences deserve particular attention. The first is the contention that, under the proposed system, richer people will be able to "get away with it": they can continue with their energy-intensive activities by buying the surplus units of lower-income people. However, this will occur only in the early years of its introduction, when buying the scarce resource of the surplus is still within their means. Moreover, the system is socially progressive as it favors those whose lifestyles are low in energy use, generally the poorer members of society: As noted earlier in this chapter, they will be able to increase their incomes by selling their surpluses. It is worth recalling that the alternative system of tackling climate change through pricing alone has the reverse effect, as poorer people have more difficulty in meeting their energy needs.

The second issue of concern stems from the difficulties that will be faced by those people who have been able to develop very "global" lives. Adapting to this may be difficult for those who have been able to maintain family and other social relationships over long distances that were not possible in the past. Likewise, politicians and their officials, people in business, the professions, sports, and culture will face problems in maintaining their current travel patterns. If the integrity of the system is to be assured, that problem can be dealt with only by people in this situation buying surplus units at the market rate but in full knowledge that their ability to do so will diminish from year to year as the allowance reduces. The fact that there is no realistic alternative to flying to reach distant destinations cannot be allowed to imply that the activity must continue. It would be facile to argue that the "need" to fly should override the needs of increasing numbers of the world's population exposed to the worsening conditions of excessive temperatures, drought, flooding, and inundation, to which flying is such a growing contributor.

CONCLUSIONS

This chapter has taken as its point of departure the contents of chapter 7, which set out the case for Contraction and Convergence as the global framework to ensure that sufficient carbon savings are made. The personal carbon allowance is the mechanism to ensure that everyone within a country is involved explicitly in meeting the imperative of reducing carbon dioxide emissions. It does so on the basis that all are entitled to an equal share of the national emissions quota.

The key points of this chapter can be summarized as:

- Personal carbon allowances would be a fair and guaranteed way of making carbon savings in each country.

- The allocation of the personal allowances would be based on the C&C principles of sharing rights to carbon dioxide emissions at the national level for coming up to half of the energy used directly by individuals.

- A system of carbon allowances would be fairer than one based on energy use and emissions by price alone and it would give a guaranteed outcome. It would promote the adoption of carbon saving as a collective goal and encourage activities that are not dependent on the use of energy. Where this is not possible, it would promote the take-up of lower or zero emission alternatives.

- Promoting a "conserver gains" in conjunction with a "polluter pays" strategy would have the effect of rewarding those who pursue lifestyles that contribute to limiting damage from climate change.

- Trading on the open market would be encouraged, with the added benefit of administrative costs being kept low.

Everyone involved, directly or indirectly, in promoting or engaging in energy-intensive lifestyles is inextricably drawn into playing down or avoiding discussion of the significance of the evidence of their contribution to climate change. That clearly cannot continue. Either the C&C concept and carbon rationing must be accepted or another realistic solution to the problem of climate change must be found — and as a matter of urgency. We have been unable to find one that stands up to the equivalent scrutiny that we have attempted to apply to the concept of carbon allowances. The following chapter discusses in further detail its application to individuals' lives.

9
CARBON WATCHERS

HOW TO LIVE
WITHIN THE
CARBON ALLOWANCE

This chapter provides the information to assess personal carbon dioxide emissions from the use of fuel in the home and in travel. It then compares current average consumption in the United States with the reductions needed to avert climate disaster. The timescale and extent of carbon reductions are discussed. Finally, guidance on how to reduce emissions is given, with further sources of advice and information listed in the appendix.

CALCULATE YOUR CARBON DIOXIDE EMISSIONS

Calculating personal carbon dioxide emissions is important to raise both individual and collective awareness of our contribution to climate change and therefore our responsibility for taking action in light of it. For most readers, such calculation will be an unfamiliar process since, apart from a couple of simple methods published on the Internet, there is no widely available method or technique for determining personal emissions, nor has government yet seen the need to provide it. However, it is a vital starting point. A "carbon literate" society will be one that helps people to live within a fair carbon allowance determined from the planet's means to absorb a safe level of greenhouse gas emissions. In our view, it is an essential first step on the road to adopting a lifestyle compatible with a stable climate. In concept, this is no different from managing our household budget so that we do not run into debt. We must now also learn to adjust our lifestyles so that we increasingly limit the energy-dependent aspects of our lives at home, at work, in our travel, and in our leisure activities.

Determining personal emissions from energy-dependent activities is likely to be a salutary learning process. In all likelihood, as a result of this exercise, you will find that you exceed the proposed future annual allowance to a considerable extent, and you will understand in some detail why this is the case. Table 2 is a simple, user-friendly tool for determining carbon dioxide emissions from the principal elements of everyday living, thereby enabling a personal

Table 2: Carbon Budgeting

(Sources: see References for chapter 9)

Annual Carbon Dioxide Emissions	Multiplier	CO_2 in kilograms		You
		Average Household	Average Individual	
ENERGY USE IN THE HOME				
Electricity (kilowatt hours)	x0.60	7,250	2,800	
Gas (kilowatt hours)	x0.19	2,330	900	
Heating Oil (gallons)	x14.20	900	350	
ENERGY USE IN TRAVEL For each mile				
Car: Standard (as driver)	x0.38			
SUV: (as driver)	x0.48	} 9,850	} 3,800	
Motorcycle: (as rider)	x0.17			
Rail: Intercity	x0.32			
Transit (light and heavy)	x0.18	} 50	} 20	

Commuter	x0.30		
Bus: Transit (city)	x0.32	} 200	} 80
Intercity	x0.06		
School	x0.09		
Bicycle	x0.00	0	0
Walking	x0.00	0	0
Air: short haul (less than 2500 miles)	x0.36	} 2,200	} 850
long haul (more than 2500 miles)	x0.39		
Ship: (such as caribbean cruise)	x1.60		
ALL for **HOME & TRAVEL** in kilograms		23,000	8,800
Share of energy use in other sectors		29,000	11,100
TOTAL CO$_2$ kilograms		52,000	20,000
TOTAL CO$_2$ tons		52	20

calculation to be made. It lists the component elements of the energy you use in your household and in your travel: the electricity, gas, and any heating oil you use, and the travel by road, rail, and air. All that needs to be done is to multiply your fuel use and mileage by the figure shown in the relevant row of the first column and record your total in the right-hand column. In the following pages we give some tips on calculating your energy use employing the multiplier for the different level of emissions of the various types of fuel.

HOUSEHOLD ENERGY USE

The majority of the energy used in the home is natural gas, electricity, and heating oil. To calculate your annual emissions you need to know how much of them your household uses each year. If you have a year's worth of your energy bills, you should be able to get a fair idea of this, even if some of your readings are estimated. The multiplier shown is for average U.S. electricity, but your local supply is likely to differ either way from this. If your utility company can supply you with information on how much carbon dioxide is actually emitted per kWh from your electricity supply, use that number instead. Consumers have little choice in the fuel mix used by their utility companies other than to opt for a green renewable tariff where that is an option.

Natural gas use can be measured in several different units at the meter, including BTUs (British thermal units), cubic meters (m^3), and kilowatt hours (kWh). Bills are typically presented in kWh, and this is the figure you need for your carbon calculation.

Electricity: multiply your annual consumption in kWh by 0.60 to establish the carbon dioxide emissions from this source in kilograms of CO2.

Natural gas: multiply your annual consumption in kWh by 0.19 to establish the carbon dioxide emissions from this source in kilograms of CO2.

Heating oil: multiply your annual consumption in gallons by 14.2 to establish the carbon dioxide emissions from this source in kilograms of CO2.

Note that current emissions per kilowatt hour from electricity are over three times those from natural gas, for reasons explained in chapter 2. If you have signed up for a green tariff, in which you receive all your electricity generated from renewable sources, then your emissions figure for electricity will be zero. If a fraction of your electricity is from fossil fuels, you should use the appropriate factor.

You then need to take each of the totals from natural gas and electricity use and for heating oil and divide them by the number of persons in the household. Put the resulting figures for yourself as an individual in the right-hand column of the table. It will be clear from this part of the exercise that the extent of personal carbon dioxide emissions from energy use in the home is critically affected by the number of people in the household. Somebody in a one-person household, regardless of income, uses around twice as much electricity and natural gas and therefore produces twice the emissions as each person in a three-person household. Thus, people in one-person households have to do considerably more to lower their emissions than those with the same lifestyle living in a multiperson household.

ENERGY USED IN TRAVEL

You now need to calculate your energy use for transportation by estimating your total annual distance traveled in miles for each of your methods of travel and then use the multiplier to establish the kilograms of carbon dioxide (kgCO2/mile). You are more likely to under- than overestimate because some journeys are easily forgotten. It is unlikely that you will know exactly how far you have traveled during the year: The aim is to get a reasonable estimate of annual travel rather than a precise figure. Table 3 gives some examples of the round-trip distances for a range of domestic and overseas destinations and the resulting average carbon dioxide emissions per passenger.

Other ways to estimate your mileage before applying the multiplier:

> **Cars:** if you have a regular service or inspection to check that your vehicle is roadworthy, you may find the mileage recorded on the last two statements, from which you can then work out your average mileage for the year. Emissions for car travel are given for the driver only in order to simplify the calculation and because fuel consumption does not rise very much when cars carry passengers.

Bus: think about how many times a week you catch the bus, if at all, and the typical length of these journeys. Calculate the total mileage, including any longer-distance bus journeys you make.

Rail: calculate the total mileage for your

Table 3. Carbon Dioxide Emissions from One Round-Trip Journey to Various Destinations

By car	Round-trip in miles	CO_2 in metric tons
Chicago–Minneapolis	820	0.31
Chicago–Washington DC	1,420	0.54
Los Angeles–Las Vegas	540	0.21
Los Angeles–San Francisco	780	0.30
Nashville–New Orleans	1,060	0.40
New York–Boston	420	0.16
New York–Washington DC	480	0.18
San Diego–Phoenix Arizona	700	0.27

By rail		
New York–Albany	320	0.10
New York–Chicago	1,620	0.52
New York–Hartford	240	0.08
Washington DC–Baltimore	80	0.03
Washington DC–Boston	900	0.29
Washington DC–New York	480	0.15

By air—domestic flight		CO_2 equivalent* in metric tons
Los Angeles–Chicago	3,500	1.26
Los Angeles–New York	4,900	2.21
Los Angeles–San Francisco	780	0.28
New York–Chicago	1,430	0.51
New York–San Francisco	5,140	2.31
San Francisco–Washington	4,880	2.20
Washington DC–Chicago	1,190	0.43
Washington DC–New York	480	0.17

(continued)

314

Table 3. (continued)

By air—international flight	Round-trip in miles	CO_2 equivalent* in metric tons
Chicago—Cape Town	16,900	6.65
Los Angeles—Manila	14,520	5.71
Los Angeles—Melbourne	15,930	6.27
Los Angeles—Tokyo	10,600	4.17
New York—London	6,900	2.71
New York—Shanghai	14,720	5.79
Washington DC—Rome	8,870	3.49
Washington DC—Sydney	19,510	7.68

The calculations for carbon dioxide emissions from air travel have been multiplied by 2.7 to take account of the warming equivalent effect of other greenhouse gases in the upper atmosphere, and are based on typical seat occupancy rates of just over 70 percent on passenger-carrying aircraft in the United States.

regular commute, longer-distance leisure travel, and use of any underground systems.

Air: for most people, air travel is infrequent enough to be memorable. Calculate the mileage of all these journeys during the last year, if any, both within the United States and overseas.

For travel by public transportation, the multiplier used is based partly on the average number of people currently using the vehicle in question: It is an average that takes account both of the relatively energy-inefficient times of the many off-peak hours, when there are few passengers, and of the peak hours, when services are much more economical in their use of fuel per passenger. The average difference in carbon dioxide emissions per passenger-mile between traveling by public transportation and by car is generally much less than might be expected. Traveling by bus in the city or by intercity or commuter rail (where the vehicles have relatively low occupancy rates) generates fairly similar emissions to traveling alone by car. However, owing to their relatively high passenger-occupancy levels, a person generates much lower emissions when making a journey by intercity bus compared with driving a car. Not surprisingly, school bus travel is very economical, too. Whereas the emissions from a car with just one driver are not dissimilar to those from air travel over the equivalent distance, the emissions are effectively halved where there is a passenger and reduced to a third with two passengers.

The significance of any journeys you make by air will be revealed in your calculation. To illustrate the point, a round-trip from Los Angeles to Tokyo for a single person accounts for the equivalent of over two tons of the carbon dioxide emissions — the same as the average *annual* emissions from each person in the current world's population for all their fossil fuel needs! Such figures indicate that the future of air travel is limited under a system that allows individuals only a fixed allowance, which if exceeded will prove increasingly expensive as it will entail buying extra allowances.

ADDING IT ALL UP

Once you have added together all the carbon dioxide emissions from your direct energy use, you will be able to compare your total with the average total for United States citizens of 9tCO2. With proper information and advice, people should learn how to use this new "currency" quickly, particularly as it will need to become such a prominent aspect of daily life.

Householders' understanding of the emissions that result from each activity would be considerably improved if they could relate those aspects of their lives that are dependent upon the use of energy to the resulting emissions. The following are suggestions for what utilities, manufacturers, and others can do to make this easier.

Smart bills and receipts: carbon dioxide

emissions recorded on electricity, natural gas, heating oil, and gasoline bills.

Smart gas and electricity meters and fuel pumps: figures of carbon dioxide emissions as well as the standard unit of consumption to be displayed.

"Carbon-ometers": a carbon dioxide counter adjacent to the odometer on the dashboard of vehicles recording details of carbon dioxide emissions.

"Carbon responsibility": carbon dioxide emissions for a journey to be included on all flight tickets and travel promotional material (such as ads in the media, outdoors, and on the Internet).

Carbon labels: energy labels on appliances and light bulbs indicating average annual emissions from one hour of use or typical annual use.

"Carbon promises": insulation materials (such as attic insulation) and home improvements (such as double glazing) recording on their packaging the carbon dioxide emissions in their production as well as energy savings made from their use in a typical house.

Carbon-rating houses and apartments: all surveyors' reports on property to include an assessment of its thermal condition, an estimate of the typical annual fuel bill for heating and hot water (and the resultant carbon dioxide emissions), and tailored advice on ways of reducing it.

"CarbonWatchers": a community information and support scheme equivalent to diet schemes such as Weight Watchers.

Based on the diet club's template, CarbonWatchers would provide its members with booklets explaining the "carbon impact" of different purchases and travel options, set reduction targets for individuals, hold regular audits (the equivalent of weigh-ins), and provide both professional and peer support for them.

INCREASING AWARENESS OF OUR CARBON DIOXIDE EMISSIONS

This book suggests that, initially, householders should be accountable only for their direct energy usage in the home and in their travel. However, it is clear that individual choices about the purchase of other goods and services also have a consequential effect through the energy required before their benefits can be gained. As the section on food in chapter 2 demonstrated, food can have a very different "indirect" energy content, depending on how and where it was grown, processed, and transported. However, as discussed earlier, attempting to include such products in an early rationing system could overload consumers with information and be difficult to establish. It is therefore not recommended for the initial years as the system is phased in. As long as businesses' emissions were controlled in an appropriate way, the prices of carbon-intensive products would increase, automatically directing consumers toward the items whose production entailed fewer emissions.

PERSONAL CARBON ALLOWANCE IN THE FUTURE

Table 4 shows both the total annual personal carbon allowance for household use and for travel (including carbon-equivalent emissions from aircraft) in the years ahead under two carbon-reducing scenarios discussed in previous chapters: one based on a carbon dioxide concentration in the atmo-

Table 4. Annual Personal Carbon Allowance Under Two Reduction Scenarios, 2009–2050

Projected carbon emissions per person tCO$_2$		Future carbon allowances, per person tCO$_2$ For all personal energy use	
		Concentration at 450 ppm	Concentration at 400 ppm
2009	9.1 (11.1)	9.1 (11.1)	9.1 (11.1)
2020	9.4 (11.5)	6.8 (8.3)	4.7 (5.7)
2030	9.9 (12.1)	4.4 (5.4)	1.1 (1.3)
2050	11.8 (14.4)	0.8 (1.0)	0.5 (0.6)

sphere not exceeding 450 ppm with convergence by 2050, and the other, a concentration of no more than 400 ppm with convergence by 2030. The system is assumed to begin in 2009, with the initial allowance set at the expected average for that year, and then decrease yearly after that date. The figure covering each individual's share of the emissions from industrial, commercial, and public-sector use for each of the years in the table is shown in parentheses.

The scale of the challenge will be appreciated by realizing that, compared with average emissions in 2009, a 450 ppm scenario would require a personal allowance of 4.4 tons by 2030 and 0.8 tons by 2050 (representing a reduction of over 90 percent). Under the 400 ppm scenario, a similar reduction will require a 1.1 tons allowance by 2030. These figures are likely to shock you, a state that will be further reinforced by comparing your own total annual emissions, established from the figures in table 2, with the graded reduction needed in the transitional years to an equal per capita allowance.

In both scenarios, the allowance shown in the table will be equal for everyone in the world: under the 450 ppm scenario, by 2050, while under the 400 ppm scenario, it will be equal by 2030. Under the 400 ppm scenario, in 2030, one return flight from New York to Miami (2,200 miles) would use most of the personal carbon allowance for the year.

It is important to recall from chapter 2 that, owing to carbon dioxide concentrations — at any level — accumulating in the atmosphere, stabilizing them requires the eventual reduction of emissions to a fraction of their current levels. So, under both scenarios, the personal carbon allowance would have to continue to fall beyond these target dates well into the future.

The figures in the table should be treated as approximate rather than precise. They rely on linear reductions (the same annual fall in emissions) and current population projections. The 450 ppm figures are based on those of the Intergovernmental Panel on Climate Change calculation that a 60 percent reduction of global emissions is needed by 2050 if the world's climate is not to be seriously destabilized. The 400 ppm figures are based on calculations by the Global Commons Institute.

Energy-use patterns have changed considerably over recent decades. There are many possibilities for reducing energy use, especially that used for travel, but they rely on the types of behavioral mileage which, since 1970, has risen at the approximate rate of 3 percent a year. Under the 400 ppm scenario, carbon dioxide emissions would have to reduce at just over double that rate. If energy efficiency and low-carbon technologies are used in conjunction with a significant reduction in motorized travel, this will not represent so great a rate of change in mobility than the United States has already experienced — it has just been in the other direction. This degree of change is not necessarily going to be easy, but it is not unrealistic.

The figures in table 4 assume that adults and children will be given equal personal carbon allowances. As mentioned briefly earlier, it is possible that the allowance would have to be lower for children so as not to advantage people with larger families. It would have to be based on evidence of the emissions currently generated in households with and without children. This would probably mean that children would then receive less than the adult allowance — possibly about half.

Climate change cannot be tackled solely by the actions of individuals. This book has emphasized the need for the world community to act together as the only possible way to limit greenhouse gas emissions sufficiently. However, it is important to realize that people are also employees, employers, students, local community activists, volunteers, members of families, friends, shareholders, voters, and citizens. In all of these roles we can affect the level of carbon dioxide emissions generated as a result of decisions made on our behalf but that can nevertheless have a major influence.

Individuals can voluntarily reduce their carbon dioxide emissions, and the advice in this chapter aims to help you contribute your share of the necessary reduction. By demonstrating that a low-carbon lifestyle is possible, you will also help in the process of convincing the wider public and the government that a lifestyle subject to a system of personal carbon allowances can work. First, you should cut down on energy-related activity; second, you should look at the options of using the energy you then use in as efficient a way as possible; and finally, you should seek to transfer your remaining needs to renewable sources. But, at least as important as "doing your bit" is supporting the movement toward a global agreement on a framework for carbon reduction, with all countries adopting the system and becoming advocates for its adoption.

How to Reduce Your Carbon Dioxide Emissions

Now that you have audited your carbon dioxide emissions, the chances are that you will wish to reduce them, either to stay within your allowance or to enjoy the benefits that might come from selling the surplus. Following are ways in which you can do this.

Personal Travel

The appendix sets out many ways to reduce the amount of energy used in your travel. In essence, it indicates that, first, you need to understand your energy use for travel. Second, it requires change in your travel patterns to substantially reduce the overall distance you travel. Third, it means making a switch to modes of transportation with low carbon dioxide emissions or to ride sharing. Finally, if car travel remains an absolute necessity, you should choose one that is as efficient as possible in terms of carbon dioxide emissions. The key advice is to travel less to lower your dependence on fossil fuels. This is particularly true for car travel but also highly relevant for extensive travel by air and public transportation. That is not to say that cutting down will be straightforward: It may need a lot of thought and planning and require years to make the necessary changes.

HOUSEHOLD ENERGY USE

The appendix also outlines many ways in which you can reduce the amount of energy used in your home. Most of them do not require major lifestyle changes or financial investment. First, you need to be familiar with the components of your household's energy consumption, including an understanding of which ones use the most and which offer the broadest scope for reduction. Information in the appendix describes how energy, particularly electricity, is used in the home. For example, the two top uses of electricity in most homes are refrigerators/freezers and air-conditioning. The only way to significantly reduce refrigerator energy is by choosing a small, efficient model when you buy a new appliance. However, the energy consumption of your air-conditioning system can be reduced significantly if you use it differently. The opportunities for saving vary considerably for different items of equipment. Second, options need to be evaluated to see where your investment might achieve the biggest reductions. Third, you need to know the wasteful actions to avoid. The appendix lists organizations and Web sites that provide detailed information on cutting down on your energy use.

INDIRECT ENERGY USE

There are other ways of saving energy as a result of decisions you make. The goods we buy come with energy "embodied" in them — that is, used in their manufacture, transportation, and retailing. Regrettably, there is little product information to enable consumers to judge whether particular products are high in embodied energy. There are general principles that, though not always applicable, can help. The appendix includes suggestions on reducing the carbon content of the food and other products you buy. Waste is another problem, owing to its embodied energy and the fact that its generation appears to be increasing at a faster rate than economic growth. Waste management can therefore contribute to your household's carbon savings. The appendix lists Web sites that provide information on these topics.

CHANGES OVER TIME

Beyond the immediate and medium-term actions you can take to reduce your personal carbon dioxide emissions, perhaps the more difficult task is to think now about adaptations for a longer-term, low-carbon future. Our proposal is that personal emissions of carbon dioxide will have to be reduced by at least 80 percent by 2030. Although energy from increased efficiency and renewable sources can help with these reductions, as seen in chapter 4, considerable changes to people's lifestyles will also be required. Many of these changes will, as we suggest later, be positive, leading to quieter and safer streets, more engagement within the local community, and so on. With the number of obese adults in the United States more than trebling since 1980, individual health should improve owing to the built-in incentive to make more journeys by non-motorized means and thereby to exercise more frequently.

Reducing dependence on motorized travel is a long-term project. Although it may be relatively straightforward to decide not to fly, or to fly less often for holidays or social reasons, or in the course of work, it will be more difficult to disentangle everyday activities from dependence on the car. Patterns of travel to work, to school, to visit relatives, to do the shopping, and for leisure all have to be rethought. In some cases, nonmotorized alternatives do not exist. If you live twenty miles from your work, for instance, cycling or walking is not possible. The question is whether in the course of time you can move closer to your job, change to a job closer to where you live, buy a more efficient or smaller car, start ride sharing, use public transportation, try to work at home for part of the week, or, if you have to commute as much as you do now, cut down on traveling for less essential reasons. Each of these responses would save a different amount of fuel and involve a different balance of costs and changes in lifestyle. There is no single correct answer. But as the allowance decreases, and the need to save energy increases, more demanding and effective steps are likely to become increasingly necessary. There will be opportunities for making considerable changes to your daily transportation patterns when you switch jobs or move to a new home. This may well be when the most substantial reductions can be achieved. We have always had to take travel considerations into account when deciding on where we live and work, for example in terms of commuting distance and proximity to family and close friends. These will become even more significant in a world in which carbon-dioxide-emitting travel has to be taken into account.

The system of carbon allowances will inevitably involve other changes in lifestyle, both welcome and unwelcome. Although people will be able to choose how to live within their allowances, and which aspects of their lives to change, given the lack of technological fixes for motorized transportation, holiday travel options are likely to narrow. At present, travel to distant locations is seen not only as a benefit in its own right but as a natural consequence of social and economic success. However, under the system, there will be much less scope for this, particularly in regard to flying.

There will be similar huge disincentives

for long-distance travel to second homes, international conferences, and regular sporting or cultural events on the calendar. However, these events are likely to continue, but with the relatively small number of active participants (whether sportspersons or musicians) making the long journeys to locations where most of the spectators or audience are local. It is very unlikely that many nonparticipants will be prepared to use a critical proportion of their allowances for these purposes, particularly if it entails flying. Alternatively, the system will lead to the necessity of reorganizing events far more at a regional or local level.

How Would the United States Look in the Late 2020s?

What would our surroundings look like, say, twenty years after the introduction of carbon allowances? These are some possibilities, most of them indicating that considerable compensations can be anticipated in aspects of our lives and environment.

Improved quality of life, both of the individual and the family, as a result of the decrease in time and costs spent in longer-distance commuting and the rise in the incidence of working from home.

331

Neighbors less likely to be strangers as a higher proportion of people's time is spent within the locality, thereby promoting community activity.

Reduction in traffic volume and speed, leading to reduced road congestion and air pollution, more pleasant travel, less danger on the roads.

Fewer deaths and injuries making travel activity more pleasant and less stressful and leading to more people on the streets on foot and bicycle.

More children out and about on their own or with friends as parental fears about the risk of injury in car crashes reduces and "stranger danger" is less of a worry as sidewalks are more populated.

Improved public transportation owing to greater demand for it.

Less road area given over to cars, both for parking and driving, thereby freeing it up for use for wider pavements, cycle lanes and cycle parking, seating, and public open space.

Far more journeys made on foot and by bicycle, leading to a healthier population as more people exercise on a daily basis, thereby improving their physical condition and well-being.

A quieter life resulting from a lowering of ambient noise levels owing to the reduction in road traffic, lower speeds, and, for those on or near flight paths, far fewer aircraft overhead.

Higher comfort levels from improving the thermal condition of housing, and more low-income people being able to pay their fuel bills.

General improvement in health due to the greater availability of local fresh food.

More energy-efficient groupings of compact housing, with fewer spread-out, low-density residential settlements.

A wider range of local shops that do not need a car to reach them and more home-delivery services.

Better resource use in the low-carbon economy as a result of greater attention being paid to minimizing the use of energy in the process of transforming raw materials into products.

Fewer oil spills and the associated pollution from accidents at sea, with less oil transported around the globe.

More trees planted throughout town and countryside as not only for aesthetic reasons but for their contribution to sequestering carbon.

An improvement in the farming landscape, with more animals in the countryside owing to the abandonment of high-energy factory farming.

More market gardening and local growing of vegetables, fruit, and flowers, owing to the need to minimize the transportation component of production.

Alternative uses found for out-of-town shopping centers and recreational activities in locations entailing long-distance travel to reach them.

At a time in history in which we now know that we must become much less energy-intensive in our lives, we have been becoming increasingly so, in most instances because we have been unaware of the consequences. Very few people indeed know the link between their fuel-based activities and the greenhouse emissions that stem from them. Understanding the contribution we are making as individuals to the forces driving this unsustainable growth in all sectors of the economy — transportation, residential, industrial, and commercial — is an essential step toward a low-carbon society. This chapter has been aimed at aiding this process. Its key elements can be summarized as:

- The provision of an easy-to-use tool that enables individuals to calculate their carbon emissions in traveling and in maintaining comfort levels in the home.
- Ensuring that global emissions remain under 400 ppm may require the personal carbon allowance in 2030 to be just 20 percent of the current average. This rate of change is not vastly differ-

ent from that experienced in personal transportation use over the last thirty years (although it is in the opposite direction).

- There are many sources of advice that can help individuals reduce their energy use and carbon dioxide emissions. However, far better "carbon information" systems are needed by consumers at the point of purchase to enable them to recognize low-energy equipment.

10
CONCLUSIONS

CLIMATE BY NEGLIGENCE OR CLIMATE BY CHOICE

We are at a historical turning point. There is now incontrovertible evidence that we are well on course to damaging the planet irreparably. It is difficult to comprehend the scale of devastation that we could bring down upon ourselves and future generations. We do know, however, that climate change will bring in its wake alarming conditions not witnessed for hundreds of thousands of years, with excessive temperatures and heat waves making life increasingly stressful, more intense and frequent storms, a destructive rise in sea levels considerably reducing the area of land for habitation, and a catastrophic loss of species. This is not a nightmare scenario portrayed by fevered environmentalists but rational analysis by climate scientists worldwide.

Economic Growth and Limiting Climate Change

What policy initiatives have been taken in light of this prospect? When the problem of climate change was first identified, "mitigation" — limiting the creation of additional climate change — was seen as an appropriate and manageable response. Since then, with escalating realization of the urgency with which global warming must be tackled, the balance has insidiously shifted toward emphasis on adaptation to a changed climate. Time is rapidly running out if we are to make the fundamental changes required to meet this greatest challenge mankind has ever faced.

The changes that are essential run counter to the way civilization has evolved since time immemorial. The need for energy in excess of human power led to innovations in farming and trading based on the strength of animals and the natural forces of wind, water, and wood. The discovery of fossil fuels over the last 250 years has vastly accelerated that process, enabling the benefits of the energy from the sun that they had accumulated over aeons to be applied in industrial activity, in transportation, and in the home. The exploitation of these finite resources has been the driving force behind increases in material standards of living, especially in the affluent West.

A reversal is required of the direction that the world has taken in its pursuit of industrial development, international trade, business activity, and tourism based on long-distance transportation. The supposition is that the profligate use of fossil fuels can continue, and that, on grounds of safeguarding the country's security of supply, especially the imports of oil from politically unstable regions of the world, the task of the U.S. administration is to expand production from more reliable locations.

We have shown that huge reductions in fossil-fuel-based activity is the key to a sufficiently effective response to climate change. Because economic growth is currently so closely linked to fossil fuel usage, this is a difficult message to accept. If economic growth is essential to our civilization, then we will have to find an alternative basis for growth very soon indeed. Chapter 8 suggested some opportunities for increasing economic activity under a low-carbon economy. However, it is clearly going to be difficult to maintain conventional economic growth as fossil fuel usage rapidly declines. In addition to finding new ways of doing business and leading our lives, we need to explore alternative measures of well-being beyond that of the GDP. These challenges, to rethink the basis on which we measure "progress" and national and personal success, and to find new opportunities for truly sustainable wealth creation, are immense. They will require bravery, creativity, and a certainty of moral purpose.

Part I explained the evidence for climate change and the serious concerns raised by continuing along a "business as usual" development path. If we carry on as we are, global average temperatures could be 10°F higher by the end of the century. Excessive use of fossil fuels; which is predicted to go on rising in the United States and worldwide, is the main cause of global warming. Individually, nationally, and internationally we have avoided confronting the reality that we must unlock ourselves from our current patterns of activity. Part II showed that technological solutions, although having considerable potential, will not provide the magic fix sufficient to reduce carbon dioxide emissions to the extent needed to prevent dangerous climate change. Meanwhile, current government action is barely scratching the surface of the problem and the search for international agreement has so far failed lamentably. Part III set out what we see as the only route to a sustainable, low-carbon future and how the strategy that this will entail is likely to affect our individual life-styles and economy as we know it.

We must learn very quickly to adjust to much more energy-thrifty and local, community-oriented patterns of activity. Our principal conclusions are:

- A massive reduction in activity based on fossil fuel use is required in order to pass on a safe environment to future generations. This can be achieved only through international agreement.
- The United States' overall contribution to a safe climate entails an 80 percent reduction in carbon dioxide emissions over the next two or three decades.
- It is wishful thinking to believe that technology — whether in the form of renewable and nuclear energy sources or improved fuel efficiency — will deliver more than a fraction of the reductions needed.
- The reductions can be achieved only by significant behavioral change.
- All energy-intensive activities will have to be significantly curtailed, in particular long-distance travel by air and road,

and wasteful practices in the home.

- A system of national personal carbon allowances should be introduced so that every individual takes responsibility for his or her emissions.
- The longer we procrastinate in taking action, the greater will be the likelihood of environmental degradation, social upheaval, and economic chaos.

CONTRACTION AND CONVERGENCE FOR NATIONS AND CARBON ALLOWANCES FOR INDIVIDUALS

We have shown that there is a fair and effective solution that can work at global, national, and individual levels to prevent the worst effects of climate change from getting out of control. It represents a realistic way out of a predicament that has resulted from years of foot dragging and failure to face up to the consequences of what we are doing.

International agreement to reduce emissions is a prerequisite for any solution to climate change. And only an equitable approach can provide the right framework to meet the challenge and to hold out any prospect of success. We have outlined what we believe is the only realistic framework for this — Contraction and Convergence

(C&C). It is based on principles of precaution and equity enshrined in the United Nations Framework Convention on Climate Change (UNFCCC). It offers a clear path for countries in both the developed and developing world through the adoption of low-carbon lifestyles and green technologies.

In effect, the safe concentration of carbon dioxide in the atmosphere sets the degree of contraction that must be achieved at the global level by the internationally agreed target date. This then determines the aggregate global emissions that have to be reduced yearly until they reach a global per capita level by that date. For the energy directly used by individuals within each country, personal carbon allowances is the proposed strategy, mirroring the logic of C&C in guaranteeing carbon savings and achieving them on a fair basis. The populations of the West are primarily responsible for the problems that climate change is increasingly causing but it is the populations of developing countries who are the first to suffer the consequences. It is therefore only fair that the former make the largest adjustments, but within a framework in which these adjustments are shared fairly across the world's population.

WHAT WE CAN DO

International negotiations take time. But there is nothing to stop a national government from introducing such a system in advance of an international agreement covering countries in both the developing and developed world. Indeed, the sooner this happens, the easier will be the transition to the inevitable low-carbon future. Climate change is too important a problem to be left solely to government, even though it has the major responsibility for dealing with it. Given the urgency with which change must occur, the active engagement of all sectors of society — politicians and the business and professional community, and, of course, individuals — is required to put pressure on government to take climate change seriously. In a democracy, the necessary intervention of government cannot take place without the consent and cooperation of the majority.

The public cannot excuse themselves for inaction on the grounds that only government action can be effective. There is no reason why individuals cannot be in the vanguard of the essential change by immediately starting to lead their lives as if they were already subject to carbon rationing. Such voluntary action would add pressure on government by showing it to be both feasible and acceptable.

If you are persuaded by the argument of this book, we suggest that you give serious consideration to the following suggestions:

At the political level:

- Tell your congressmen, senator, mayor, etc., and those running for office of your concerns about climate change and ask them what they are doing about it.
- Ask what commitment on the subject they are making or will make if elected.
- Get involved in debates on the actions that need to be taken to prevent climate change.

At the personal level:

- Complete the carbon dioxide emissions self-audit in chapter 9. Then compare your annual total with the average of the world's annual per capita emissions of four tons and the average of less than one and a half tons that we must get down to as speedily as possible.
- In light of the marked contrast that this is very likely to reveal, set an an-

nual target for reducing your carbon dioxide emissions, using the table in the same chapter, and monitor your progress.

- Take advantage of the many sources of information about how to reduce household energy and your use and dependence on motorized travel such as those listed in the appendix.
- Discuss with your friends and family your concerns about climate change and the types of action that can be taken.
- Join or support an environmental group engaged with this issue and encourage community organizations, religious groups, and so on, to do so as well.

OUR MORAL CHOICE

Responding to climate change is ultimately a moral choice. The implications of failure to limit our emissions to a fair share dictated by the planet's capacity to safely absorb greenhouse gas emissions are dire. We can no longer proceed as if we have an inalienable right to ignore the damage we are causing to the planet. Nor can we keep passing the buck between individuals, industry, and government. If we are to genuinely support the rights of our children to inherit a healthy planet, we must stop pretending that the harm we are causing is marginal. The carbon dioxide emissions that we are adding to the atmosphere will affect the climate for hundreds of years. It is indefensible to make decisions that we know will prejudice the prospects of future generations enjoying life on earth. Yet, we are heading inexorably in that direction.

We have a fundamental and collective responsibility to act with this inescapable truth in mind. Future generations will justifiably sit in judgment on what current generations chose to do in full knowledge of the devastating consequences of continuing with our energy-profligate lifestyles. We are all as individuals to varying degrees complicit in a process that is already reducing the quality of life of literally *millions* of people and will almost certainly cause the deaths of *millions* in the near and longer-term future. The only strategy now open to government can be to act resolutely to slow the pace of damaging change. The accumulation of evidence on climate change and its damaging impacts makes it progressively unacceptable that we attempt to plead ignorance with the excuse "we did not know" — with all its haunting World War II images of the outcome of looking the other way.

APPENDIX

There are many ways to substantially reduce your energy use right now. Many do not require major lifestyle changes or financial investment. Here are some steps you can take when you travel, in your household, and in other choices you make.

In addition, there are a number of online Carbon Calculators that can give you an indication of your total carbon emissions. Examples of such calculators are located at:

Safe Climate: www.safeclimate.net/calculator

Fight Global Warming: www.fightglobalwarming.com/

Climate Crisis: www.climatecrisis.net/takeaction/carboncalculator

Understand Your Travel Energy Use

Write a travel diary for a week or a month-, for yourself and for the rest of your household. Include walking and cycling. Note the day, time, origin, destination, and aim of each journey you make, the distance traveled, method of transportation used, cost, and trip time. The results will give you insights into how and why you make each journey, particularly those by air and regular long-distance ones by car. This information will help you prioritize changes.

Change Your Travel Patterns

Although short journeys are more easily made by nonmotorized methods, remember that in the end, total distance traveled is the crucial determinant of your carbon dioxide emissions. You could:

- Cut down as much as possible on air travel. From a climate change perspective, it is by far the most damaging of your activities, not least because of the sheer distance of journeys. More savings can be made by cutting out one long flight than dozens of car journeys. Taking a vacation closer to home so that you do not have to fly may be the single most important thing you can do.

- Find out more about local public transportation options and ride-sharing for commuting.
- Use the school bus or join a car pool with other local families to reduce the school-run traffic.
- Choose local shops and services whenever you can, and try to combine several purposes in one trip. You will save time and money as well.
- If you have a teenager keen to get a driver's license, make him or her pay for the lessons, and try giving an incentive not to drive, such as a higher allowance if public transportation, the school bus, a car pool, or a bicycle is used.
- If you have a teenager who insists on driving, make him or her contribute to the costs of the gasoline and servicing of the car.
- Set yourself an achievable fuel-reduction target for the year (say down from one thousand to five hundred miles a month) and regularly monitor your progress. Make the target more ambitious each year and watch your spending on gasoline drop.

- Walk on short trips and cycle on medium-length trips instead of using a car.

Reduce Fuel Use in Your Car

- Plan ahead: whenever you can, choose uncongested routes, combine trips, and ride share.
- Cold starts: drive off as soon as possible after starting.
- Drive smoothly and efficiently: harsh acceleration and heavy braking have a significant effect on fuel consumption; driving smoothly saves fuel.
- Do not drive at high speeds as this increases fuel consumption: driving at 70 mph uses 30 percent more fuel than driving at 50 mph.
- If you have a manual transmission, use higher gears as soon as traffic conditions allow.
- Switch off the engine whenever it is safe to do so.
- Don't carry unnecessary weight in the trunk, and remove roof racks when not in use.
- Regular servicing helps keep the engine at best efficiency and minimizes fuel consumption, as does maintaining

tires at the correct pressure.

- Use air-conditioning in your car sparingly since it increases fuel consumption significantly.

TRANSPORTATION AND ENERGY WEB SITES

The organizations in the United States listed below provide details of online resources and information to help you make carbon-informed lifestyle changes related to your travel. In addition, state and district Web sites are likely to have useful information about public transportation networks, ride-sharing, and cycling. In particular, look for information about tax credit programs available to employers and commuters to encourage reducing work-related travel mileage. For example, Maryland has a tax credit program that allows businesses to claim a 50 percent tax credit for the cost of providing commuter fringe benefits to its employees.

Alternative Fuels Data Center focuses on alternative-fuel vehicles and has a site with a search database of commercially available vehicles by category and an alternative fuels station locator. (www.eere .energy.gov/afdc)

Best Workplaces for Commuters SM is a new public-private sector voluntary program advocating employer-provided commuter benefits. (www.commuterchoice.gov)

Better World Club (www.betterworld club.com), **Carbon Neutral** (www.carbon neutral.com) and **Climate Care** (www .climatecare.org) are companies that aim to help offset the greenhouse gas pollution associated with travel through an online payment used to invest in projects mostly in developing countries, such as clean energy and forestry. However, as chapter 4 showed, this can have only a limited role in reducing emissions. On the Carbon Neutral Web site is a carbon calculator for you to work out your emissions.

CALSTART's Advanced Transportation provides up-to-date information on electric, natural gas, hybrid electric vehicles, and intelligent transportation technologies. (www.calstart.org)

Car Sharing Network is a resource for finding out about ride-sharing schemes and carpool clubs in your community. (www.car sharing.net/where.html)

Choose Climate is a site that explains the climate change issues concerning air travel and allows calculations to be made of emissions from particular flights. It also has suggestions for alternative methods of transportation. (www.chooseclimate.org)

Department of Energy provides a simple Web-based tool to determine the fuel efficiency of new and used cars in miles per gallon and greenhouse gases. (www.fuel economy.org)

Drive Clean in California is a "zero and near-zero emission vehicle guide" from the California Air Resources Board with facts and news about clean cars. (www.drive clean.ca.gov)

Environmental Defense's Tailpipe Tally is an online tool that enables you to calculate, from your mileage or even just the year and make of your car, how much your vehicle pollutes. (www.environmental defense.org/tailpipetally)

Environmental Protection Agency (EPA) and the U.S. Department of Transportation (DOT) have set up the Commuter Choice Leadership Initiative to work with businesses to limit the damage from commuting by car. (www.commuterchoice.gov)

Federal Highway Administration has a Bike and Pedestrian Program run by its Office of Human and Natural Resources to promote the safety of cyclists and pedestrians. (www.fhwa.dot.gov/environment/bike ped)

Fuel Economy Web Site is an online tool enabling you to compare miles per gallon ratings as well as corresponding greenhouse gas emissions from all model year 2000 vehicles onwards. (www.fueleconomy.gov).

Green Books has published a useful little book — *Cutting Your Car Use: Save Money, Be Healthy, Be Green* — with helpful hints and tips, case studies, and success stories, together with tables that help you work out how much money you can save by using your car less or giving it up altogether. (tel. +011 (44) 1803 863260; www.green books.co.uk)

Green Guide to Cars and Trucks is a ranking of cars and trucks according to their environmental friendliness, provided by the American Council for an Energy-Efficient

Economy (ACEEE). (www.greenercars
.com)

Office of Transportation Technologies
provides information about alternative fuel
and advanced transportation technologies,
including hybrids, as well as performance
reports and other research. (www1.eere
.energy.gov/vehiclesandfuels)

**Pedestrian and Bicycle Information
Centre** provides resources for learning
about cycling and walking and advises on
facilities in your neighborhood. (www
.walkinginfo.org)

**Transportation Action Network
(TransAct)** provides information and
resources for people working to make their
communities better places to live in by
reducing traffic. (www.transact.org)

HOUSEHOLD ENERGY USE

Understand Your Household's Energy Consumption

Having looked at your annual energy consumption in order to audit your carbon
dioxide emissions, consider in more detail
how that energy is used so that you can
identify the major opportunities for saving.

The amount used for different purposes depends very much on your home and lifestyle. Far more energy is used in maintaining comfort levels in the home than is used for lighting and the use of appliances.

Save Energy Used in Heating and Hot Water

The average U.S. household with gas central heating uses 70 percent for space heating, 28 percent for water heating, and 2 percent for cooking. Similar proportions apply to other fuels. The most cost-effective improvements both in terms of energy saved and payback on investment depend on your property and circumstances. A more efficient or newer house will use less energy for heating than a large, inefficient or old house, and the more people in a household, the less energy per person is needed. Where applicable, the following options are likely to be the most worthwhile:

- Sign up for a green tariff (electricity generated from renewable sources) from your utility company if one is available.
- Fit additional loft insulation. Most houses now have some, but increasing

its thickness is one of the most cost-effective ways of saving energy. You can fit it yourself or have it done by a professional. And your energy company/local authority may offer subsidies or discounts.

- If you have unfilled cavity walls, get them insulated. This could save up to a third of your heating bills and will pay back the investment within a few years.
- To cut down on heat loss, other home improvements include draft proofing; fitting shelves above radiators under windows; placing reflective foil behind radiators on external walls; insulating hot-water pipes; and putting up thermally lined curtains. (And, of course, do not open windows to cool an overheated home in winter.)
- Solar water-heating systems, though requiring an initial investment, run on renewable energy and can save up to half your hot-water bills. There are several companies that install these, and in some areas there is support for people who want to do it themselves.
- Other, more expensive options include photovoltaic and geothermal energy. There are grants and subsidies avail-

able that can help offset the cost of installing them.

- When replacing your windows, invest in a more efficient type. Double glazing is now becoming standard, but for nearly all homes you could consider "low-e" glass (which saves more energy) or triple glazing, particularly for rooms kept at warmer temperatures.

- If you are buying a new furnace, talk to your plumber about getting a condensing boiler. These are around 90 percent efficient compared with around 80 percent for a conventional new one, or 65 percent for the average one currently in use.

- Burning wood to heat your home is another renewable-energy option. An EPA certified wood-burning stove produces only two to five grams of smoke per hour compared to ten times as much in older, uncertified wood-stoves and fireplaces. But wood requires considerable storage space and in a poorly insulated home will not provide a large proportion of heating energy. In a ranking of options based on carbon saved per pound invested, woodstoves are likely to come below most insulation improvements. Nevertheless, it is one of very few options available for renewable heating energy. (By contrast, burning coal or smokeless fuel in an open fire is probably the highest-carbon emitting option because coal is carbon-intensive and open fires are very inefficient.) Learning to better use the controls on your heating and hot-water system will also help you to save energy and money. It can also be very worthwhile to have controls fitted if you do not already have them.

- Most furnaces have timers that enable you to control when your system switches on. To save energy, experiment with turning it off well before you go to bed — the better insulated your home is, the longer it will take to cool down, but it should stay warm enough for at least thirty minutes. Switching off heating half an hour earlier could save over 5 percent of your energy bill.

- A hot-water thermostat controls the temperature of stored hot water and should not be set higher than 140°F (both to prevent scalding and to save energy).

- Thermostats set the temperature in homes or in individual rooms. As a rule of thumb, for each 2°F lower you set the thermostat, you save 10 percent of heating energy. You will have to make your own judgment in the winter on the balance between saving energy, wearing warm clothing, and personal comfort.
- A water-saving shower head or a water-flow restrictor fitted to a standard or power shower can save money and energy while still providing a good-quality shower. However, the nontechnological options can be more effective: You can save energy by having cooler and quicker showers and baths. Cutting just two minutes off your shower time can save a quarter of the energy used.
- Bathing and showering: The hot water used for this depends on the temperature of the water, how much you use, and how often. These are all things you can control. In a comparison between having a bath and a five-minute shower, perhaps surprisingly the power shower uses more water, typically twenty-five gallons, the bath and standard shower use five to fifteen gallons,

an aerating shower (which saves water and energy by adding air to the mix), and an electric shower use approximately ten gallons or less in five minutes. As the average time spent in the shower is nearer seven to eight minutes, in fact only aerating and electric showers use less water than a bath.

Save Energy Used on Cooling Your Home

- Air-conditioner units: As with central heating systems, having thermostats and timing controls will greatly improve energy savings.
- Use the unit only when the outside temperature is higher than 78°F — setting the thermostat down to 72°F increases cooling costs by 12 to 47 percent, depending on where you live.
- To reduce your needs for cooling, close windows and draw drapes and shades during daytime to keep out heat.
- At night, open the windows and turn on window or attic fans to draw in the cooler air. In addition, passive cooling techniques such as shading, ventilation, and vegetation can reduce cooling needs.
- To avoid wasting energy, set the unit to come on half an hour before you

get home.

- Regular maintenance, including keeping filters clean, will also cut energy consumption.
- If you have a central air-conditioning unit, make sure the ducts are properly insulated, especially those in the attic or any other unconditioned area.
- It is important to install the unit in a shaded spot with unrestricted air circulation around it and on the house's north or eastside, because direct sunshine on its outdoor heat exchanger decreases efficiency.
- If your unit is exposed to the sun, a shading device such as an awning can protect it.
- Units should be fitted snuggly in a window to prevent any cool air from leaking to the outside.
- Both unit and central air conditioners have bright yellow Energy-Guide labels that provide information on their energy efficiency in large black numbers.
- Ceiling fans: Substituting fans for air-conditioning can save well over half the energy costs. It is often also worthwhile to replace any conventional fan with a far more energy efficient Energy Star

model. Make sure you turn it off when you are not in the room.

- A sun room may help to keep homes warmer in the autumn and spring but are incredibly wasteful to heat in winter. Patio heaters are even worse.

SAVE ENERGY USED FOR APPLIANCES AND LIGHTS

- Buy products that are of better quality, likely to have a longer life, and repairable. Owning fewer but longer-lasting objects throughout your life will be less energy-intensive than having to buy frequent replacements.
- When replacing refrigerators, freezers, washing machines, dryers, dishwashers, electric ovens, and light bulbs, make sure that you buy energy-efficient models. Energy labels are on all these appliances. However, remember that energy consumption is more important than energy efficiency. A large, efficient refrigerator/freezer may use more energy than a smaller, less efficient one.
- Washing machine: Detergents have been developed to work just as effectively in cold water as in hot water, so switch from hot to warm or cold water, thereby saving 40 percent of

energy needed per cycle. Most people underload their washing machines. A washing machine is made for loads of ten to eleven pounds, so aim to cut down the number of cycles by using it to full capacity.

- Supplying "hot fill" water to the washing machine from a source heated by gas rather than its own electric heater will reduce the need for energy. The savings will be much greater with an Energy Star model that uses only eighteen to twenty-five gallons per cycle compared with standard washing machines, which typically use forty gallons of water per cycle.

- Dishwasher: As with washing machines, lower-temperature cycles save energy and, together with fully loading your dishwasher, will reduce the number of times it is run. Washing dishes by hand may lower emissions but only if you restrict the flow of hot water to avoid wasting it. When you next buy a dishwasher, buy the right size for your home: A standard-capacity model typically holds more than eight place settings, whereas a compact-capacity model may be sufficient.

- Cook in a microwave instead of a

conventional oven, put lids on pans of boiling water, do not preheat the oven in advance of when you need it, and, for electric burners use unwarped cooking pans with good surface contact.

- Refrigerator and freezer: Removing dust from any exposed cooling coils at their backs, and not putting hot or even warm food into them, and defrosting the freezer regularly, save energy.

- Home electronics: The average home in the United States has roughly two TVs, a VCR, a DVD player, and two or three telephones. Most of the electricity used to power them is consumed while the products are turned off unless you unplug them. A standby switch left on uses about 70 W per home — that is about 600 kWh a year (more than that used by most new refrigerators). When you have to replace appliances, buy ones with the electronics of Energy Star models.

- Equipment chargers: These also use energy when plugged in, even when nothing is attached.

- Switch off the microwave completely when not in use, as, during the year, a similar amount of energy is required to power its electronic clock display as is used for cooking.

- Lighting: Install energy-saving light bulbs (technically known as compact fluorescent lamps or CFLs). Fitting them in the four most used locations in the average home can save 200 kWh each year, which is more than a quarter of the electricity typically used for lighting in the home. CFL bulbs, available in a range of sizes and designs, cost in the range of four to fifteen dollars per bulb and save about twenty-five to thirty dollars per bulb in fuel bills over its lifetime. They also last — around ten times longer than conventional ones. As with all bulbs, switch them off when they are not needed.

- Do not have a 300–500 W security light switching on all the time outside your house. (If you need a security light, there are efficient alternatives.)

- Do not buy a large, frost-free refrigerator/freezer or a power shower, leaf blower, or ride-on lawnmower — all are wasteful of energy.

Organizations in the United States listed below provide details of online resources and information on how you can save energy in your household. Also, contact your energy company. Most have energy-savings brochures and offer a free home-energy survey. In order to help meet required state energy-savings targets, your energy company may provide financial incentives for you to take up energy-efficiency measures, such as cavity wall insulation, top-up loft insulation, and energy-saving light bulbs.

Alliance to Save Energy is a coalition of business, government, environmental, and consumer leaders who are promoting efficient and clean energy use worldwide. The site has lots of helpful tips, plus you can sign up to receive its news bulletin on your e-mail account. (www.ase.org)

The American Council for an Energy-Efficient Economy (ACEEE) is a very good site if you are looking for technical and policy-related materials on energy efficiency. (www.aceee.org)

CEERT is a site with lots of information on energy efficiency, renewable energy, and sustainable technology information and connections. The site is developed by the Center for Energy Efficiency and Renewable Technologies. (www.ceert.org)

Center for Energy Efficiency & Renewable Technologies has a site with information on technologies relevant to its title. (www.cleanpower.org)

Consumer Energy Center provides information to help you make smart energy choices. (www.consumerenergycenter.org)

Database of State Incentives for Renewable Energy (DSIRE) is a comprehensive source of information on state, local, utility, and selected federal incentive programs to promote renewable energy. (www.dsire usa.org)

Environmental Protection Agency (EPA) has an Energy Star Program in collaboration with the Department of Energy and many companies aimed at helping consumers buy products that use less energy. Its coverage includes electrical appliances, lighting, TVs and VCRs, heating, cooling, office equipment, and even new homes. Details on the total energy consumption of appliances are given on the energy label. There is a search facility to enable you to locate the nearest store to you that will supply different household products and appliances available on the market with the Energy Star label. (www.energy star.gov) The Energy Star Home Improvement Toolbox is an online tool to help you identify opportunities for saving money and energy around your house. (www.energy star.gov/home improvement) You could visit Emission Profiler, where you can learn how much carbon dioxide, sulfur dioxide, and nitrogen oxide emissions are produced to generate electricity in your state, and if you enter information about your electricity consumption — which you will find on your energy bills — you can get your household emissions calculated for you. (www.epa.gov/cleanenergy/powerprofiler.htm) You can also visit this site to get information on wood-stoves and a list of this certified by EPA. (www.epa.gov/woodstoves)

Green Power Partnership, together with the EPA, has created a green-power locator of energy services using electricity generated from landfill gas, biomass, or wind power. (www.epa.gov/greenpower/locator/)

Home Energy Saver is another online tool that identifies ways in which you can save an average of five hundred dollars annually in energy bills by simply entering your Zip code and some details about your home. The tool is developed by Lawrence Berkeley Lab's Energy Advisor program. The site gives you the resources you need to make it happen. (http://hes.lbl.gov)

Lawrence Berkeley National Laboratory-Environmental Energy Technologies has lots of information about building standards, energy analysis, and the indoor environment. (http://eetd.lbl.gov)

National Center for Photovoltaics is a searchable Web page from the Department of Energy with information on photovoltaic (e.g., solar cells). (www.nrel.gov/ncpv)

Northeast Energy Efficiency Partnerships (NEEP) is a nonprofit regional organization dedicated to increasing and coordinating energy-efficiency efforts in New England, New York, and the mid-Atlantic region. (www.neep.org)

Power Scorecard is an online tool that helps consumers in California and Pennsylvania choose power generated from clean sources such as wind and sun. (www.power score.org)

Power Profiler is an online tool you can use to generate a report about electricity use and the resulting emissions — all you need is your Zip code. (www.epa.gov/clean energy/powerprofiler.htm)

Renewable Northwest Project is a coalition of public-interest organizations and energy companies working to promote renewable energy. There is information about switching to green electricity in the Northwest. (www.rnp.org)

The Rocky Mountain Institute has a Community Energy Opportunity Finder resource, which is an interactive tool that will help you determine your community's best bets for energy solutions that benefit the local economy, the community, and the environment. (www.energyfinder.org/)

San Diego Gas & Electric Company site has lots of easy-to-use energy-efficiency information for householders. (www.sdge.com)

Indirect Energy Use

There are other, more indirect ways of making informed lifestyle changes to reduce your energy use, such as when and what food you buy, minimizing household waste, and making more use of renewable energy.

- For food and drinks, use the "country of origin" information to choose those that were grown or produced closer to your home, thereby reducing your "food-miles" and hence your carbon dioxide emissions. Likewise, consider buying organic food, especially that which is grown locally. And choose more seasonal foods, which are less likely to have been grown either far away or in heated greenhouses.
- Find out about your local farmers' market, farm shops, or vegetable box scheme, all of which can supply local, fresh food. (www.foodroutes.org/localfood)
- Buy recycled products or those with high recycled content, such as paper products made with "postconsumer" waste.

- Use nondisposable products as much as possible: for example rechargeable batteries, or your own shopping bag rather than hundreds of disposable plastic bags each year.

There are also many ways in which you can manage the waste from your household in order to save energy. These are outlined below:

- Compost your vegetable and garden waste if you have a garden. Alternatively, use a wormery: an easy and efficient system of converting ordinary kitchen waste into top-quality compost and concentrated liquid feed through the natural action of worms.
- Recycle rather than dispose of your waste: Door-to-door collections of recyclable material or local recycling banks now exist in most urban areas. But avoid compromising the carbon-saving benefits of recycling by making special trips by car to deliver them! In addition, some charities accept special items such as mobile phones and printer cartridges for recycling or reuse.
- Your local authority may have pro-

duced a guide on recycling waste and offer advice on composting as well as discounts on compost bins.

Non-government Organizations

Environmental Defense Fund is a membership organization that links science, economics, and law to create equitable and cost-effective solutions for addressing major environmental problems. (www.environ mentaldefense.org)

Natural Resource Defense Council (NRDC) is an environmental-action organization campaigning on a variety of major environmental issues including climate change. It has more than 1.2 million members. (www.nrdc.org)

Redefining Progress works with a broad range of partners to shift the economy and public policy toward sustainability. They use tools such as Ecological Footprinting and Genuine Progress Indicators as well as developing new frameworks such as Common Assets. (www.rprogress.org)

Pew Center on Global Climate Change was set up in the late 1990s as a nonprofit, nonpartisan, independent organization. The center provides information about global climate change as well as solutions for addressing this issue. (www.pewclimate.org)

Resources for the Future is an environmental think tank focused on improving environmental and natural-resource policymaking worldwide through objective social science research. (www.rff.org)

Rocky Mountain Institute is an entrepreneurial nonprofit organization that fosters the efficient and restorative use of resources to make the world secure, prosperous, and life-sustaining. The institute's efforts are focused on designing inspiring integrative solutions that can be adopted and developed by business, civil society, and government. (www.rmi.org)

World Resources Institute is an environmental think tank that works to put research into action. The organization works in a number of areas including ecosystem services, climate change, markets and enterprises, and governance. An excellent tool provided by WRI is Earth Trends, an environmental information portal, which has lots of useful data on a wide range of topics, including energy and climate. (www.wri.org); (www.earthtrends.org)

OTHER USEFUL WEB SITES

The organizations in the United States listed below provide details of online resources and information on how you can calculate your carbon emissions and support carbon-saving projects. It also includes the names of institutes and other bodies active in related research and campaigning.

Environmental Protection Agency (EPA) has a Landfill Methane Outreach Program to help businesses, states, energy providers, and communities develop landfill methane projects, thereby creating a clean energy alternative to fossil fuels. (www.epa .gov/lmop)

Grist **magazine** is an online environmental magazine giving you the lowdown on many hot-topic issues. You can have the highlight news stories sent daily or weekly to your e-mail account. (www.grist.org)

ABBREVIATIONS USED IN THIS BOOK

The following abbreviations and acronyms have been used throughout:

Units of Measure
BTUs British thermal units
GtC gigaton (thousand million metric tons) of carbon
GWh gigawatt (thousand million watt) hours
kgC kilograms of carbon
kgCO2 kilograms of carbon dioxide
kWh kilowatt hours
MtC million tons of carbon
mtoe million tons of oil equivalent
MW megawatt (1 million watts)
ppm parts per million
tC tons of carbon
tCO2 tons of carbon dioxide
toe tons of oil equivalent

Other Abbreviated Terms and Acronyms
AIP Airport Improvement Program
C&C contraction and convergence
CFL compact fluorescent lamps
CHP combined heat and power
COP Conference of the Parties to the Convention on Climate Change
DSIRE Database of State Incentives for Renewable Energy
DTQ Domestic Tradable Quotas

FSU Former Soviet Union countries
GDP gross domestic product
ISTEA Intermodal Surface Transportation Act
LPG liquid petroleum gas
MEP Member of the European Parliament
NGO non-government organization
PV photovoltaics
RECS Renewable Energy Consumption Survey
RGGI Regional Greenhouse Gas Initiative
RPS Renewable Portfolio Standards
SBC System Benefits Charge
TEA Transportation Equity Act
VAT value added tax

Organizations
ACEEE American Council for Energy-Efficiency Economy
CEPS Centre for European Policy Studies
CREST Center for Renewable Energy and Sustainable Technology
DEFRA Department for Environment, Food and Rural Affairs in the UK
DETR Department for the Environment, Transport and the Regions in the UK
DOE U.S. Department of Energy
DOT U.S. Department of Transportation
ECI Environmental Change Institute, Oxford, UK

EIA Energy Information Administration
EPA Environmental Protection Agency
EU European Union
FHWA Federal Highway Administration
GCI Global Commons Institute, UK
IEA International Energy Agency
IPCC Intergovernmental Panel on Climate Change
IPPR Institute for Public Policy Research, UK
NEEP Northeast Energy Efficiency Partnership
NEF National Energy Foundation
NRDC Natural Resources Defense Council
OECD Organization for Economic Co-operation and Development
OPEC Organization of Petroleum Exporting Countries
PIU Performance and Innovation Unit (UK Government Cabinet Office)
ORCAS Oak Ridge Center for Advanced Studies
ORNL Oak Ridge National Laboratory
PSI Policy Studies Institute, London
RCEP Royal Commission on Environmental Pollution, UK
SDC Sustainable Development Commission, UK
UNEP United Nations Environment Programme

WBGU German Scientific Advisory Council on Global Environmental Change
WCED World Council on Environment and Development
WHO World Health Organization
WRI World Resources Institute
WWI WorldWatch Institute

REFERENCES

References are arranged alphabetically by "author," whether an individual or an organization. Organizations referred to in the main text can usually be located in the references, even if the work is listed under the name of an individual. In those few cases where it might be difficult to trace a source, the issue mentioned in the text is set in parentheses after the reference.

INTRODUCTION

Gore, Al. *Earth in the Balance: Ecology and the Human Spirit.* New York: Plume Books, 1993.

1. BEYOND THE PLANET'S LIMITS

Athanasiou, T., and P. Baer. *Dead Heat: Global Justice and Global Warming.* New York: Seven Stories Press, 2002.

BBC TV. *Horizon,* 13 January 2005.

BBC Radio 4 *News.* "North Pole Ice 'Turns to Water.' " 20 August 2000. news.bbc.co .uk/1/hi/world/americas/888235.stm.

Campbell-Lendrum, D., C. F. Corvalan, and A. Prus-Ustun. "How much disease could climate change cause?" In Mc-Michael, A. J., D. H. Campbell-Lendrum, C. F. Corvalan, K. L. Ebi, A. K. Githeko, J. D. Scheraga, and A. Woodward, eds. *Climate Change and Human Health: Risks and Responses.* Geneva: WHO, 2003.

Clarke, T. "Holistic Model Hints Next Century Could Get Even Hotter Than We Thought." *Nature Science Update,* 23 May 2003. www.nature.com/nsu/030519/030519–9.html.

Cox, P. M., R. A. Betts, C. D. Jones, S. A. Spal, and I. J. Totterdell. "Acceleration of Global Warming Due to Carbon-cycle Feedbacks in a Coupled Climate Model." *Nature* 408, 9 November 2000.

Conisbee, M., and A. Simms. *Environmental Refugees: The Case for Recognition.* London: New Economics Foundation, 2003.

Environmental Protection Agency. Reports on *The U.S. Greenhouse Gas Inventory, Coastal Erosion,* and the *U.S. Climate Action Report,* 2002. http://yosemite.epa.gov/oar/globalwarming.nsf/content/Resource

CenterPublicationsUSClimateAction
Report.html.

Flannery, T. *The Weather Makers: The History and Future Impact of Climate Change.* England: Allen Lane, 2006.

Griggs, K. "New Zealand's Belching Animals." BBC News, 7 May 2002. www.news.bbc.co.uk/2/hi/science/nature/1972621.stm.

Houghton, J. *Global Warming: The Complete Briefing.* England: Cambridge University Press, 2004.

Inhofe, James, M., chair of the U.S. Senate Environment and Public Works Committee. 28 July 2003 (Science of Climate Change Statement describing global warming as a hoax).

Intergovernmental Panel on Climate Change. Watson, R. T., and the Core Writing Team, eds. *Climate Change 2001: The Synthesis Report: A Contribution of Working Groups I, II and III to the Third Assessment Report of the IPCC.* England: Cambridge University Press, 2001.

International Energy Agency. *Global CO2 Emissions from Fuel Consumption,* 2004.

International Scientific Steering Committee (ISSC). *Report of the International Symposium on the Stabilisation of Greenhouse*

Gas Concentrations. Exeter: Hadley Centre, Met Office, 2005.

Jones, P., and J. Palutikof. "Global Temperature Record." Climate Research Unit and UK Meteorological Office, Hadley Centre (Original copy of graph reproduced as figure 3). http://www.cru.uea.ac.uk/cru/info/warming/.

Kansas City Star. Report on scientists report on the spread northwards of several small mammals' habitat during the last century. 8 Dec 2005.

Kasting, J. F. "The Carbon Cycle, Climate and Long-term Effects of Fossil Fuel Burning," 2001. http://www.gcrio.org/CONSEQUENCES/vol4no1/carbcycle.html.

Keeling, C. D., and T. P. Whorf. "Atmospheric CO2 Records from Sites in the SIO Air Sampling Network." In *Trends: a Compendium of Data on Global Change.* Carbon Dioxide Information Analysis Center, Oak Ridge National Laboratory, U.S. Department of Energy, 2005.

Kirpotin, S., and J. Marquand. Oxford University study on methane release in Western Siberia reported. *New Scientist,* 11 August 2005.

Larsen, J. *Record Heat Wave in Europe Takes 35,000 Lives.* Earth Policy Institute Eco-

Economy Update. Washington, DC, October 2003.

Long, Charles N., et al. "Changes in Earth's Reflectivity." *Science* 308, 2005.

Lynas, Mark. *Six Degrees.* New York: Fourth Estate, in press.

Marland, G., T. Boden, and R. J. Andres. "Global, Regional, and National CO2 Emissions." In *Trends: a Compendium of Data on Global Change.* Carbon Dioxide Information Analysis Center, Oak Ridge National Laboratory, U.S. Department of Energy, 2006.

Munich Re. *Topics 2000: Natural Catastrophes — The Current Position.* Munich: Munich Re-insurance Company, 2000.

Myers, Norman. *Environmental Refugees: An Emergent Security Issue.* Prague: 13th Economic Forum, May 2005.

NASA Earth Observatory. Report on desertification. In *Media Alerts Archive,* 16 June 2005.

National Academy of Sciences, Division of Earth Sciences, Committee on Climatology. T. F. Malone, chair. *First General Report on Climatology to the Chief of the Weather Bureau.* Washington, DC, 1957 (on risks of excessive fossil fuel consumption).

National Academy of Sciences. *Proceedings* 102, no. 31, 25 July 2005 (on drought affecting different parts of the world).

National Assessment Synthesis Team 2000. *Climate Change Impacts on the United States.* http://www.usgcrp.gov/usgcrp/Library/nationalassessment/overview.htm.

Norris, S., R. Rosentrater, and P. M. Eid. *Polar Bears at Risk.* Gland, Switzerland: WWF — World Wide Fund for Nature, 2002.

Ocean and Climate Change Institute, Woods Hole Oceanographic Institution (reports on tropical storm activity).

Press Association. "Global Warming Could Trigger Mass Extinction." *Guardian,* 19 June 2003.

Sample, I. "Not Just Warmer, It's the Hottest for 2,000 Years." *Guardian,* 1 September 2003.

Schellnhuber, J. ed. *Avoiding Dangerous Climate Change.* England: Cambridge University Press, 2006.

Science and Technology Committee. *Scientific Advisory System: Scientific Advice on Climate Change.* London: Third report, House of Commons, 2000.

Union of Concerned Scientists (report on climate change skeptics), www.ucsusa.org.

United Nations Framework Convention on

Climate Change. New York: UN, 1992.

Webster, P. J., G. J. Holland, J. A. Curry, and H. R. Chang. "Changes in Tropical Cyclone Number, Duration, and Intensity in a Warming Environment." *Science* 309, September 2005.

www.epa.gov/globalwarming/publications/ emissions. Data are for 2003.

Zhang, K., B. C. Douglas, and S. Leatherman. "Global Warming and Coastal Erosion." In *Climatic Change* 64, nos. 1 and 2, May 2004.

2. As If There's No Tomorrow

Aviation Environment Federation. *Fly Now, Grieve Later.* June 2005 (on aviation habits in the United States).

BBC Radio 4 *News,* news item on nuclear fusion, 28 June 2005. news.bbc.co.uk/1/hi/ sci/tech/4629239.stm#.

BP. *BP Statistical Review of World Energy, 2006.* www.bp.com.

Centers for Disease Control and Prevention (on adult obesity in the United States).

Centre for Environmental Strategy. *UK Carbon Attribution Model.* Surrey University: 2005.

Davis, S. C., and S. W. Diegel. *Transportation Energy Data Book,* edition 24. Tennessee: Oak Ridge National Laboratory (on U.S. vehicle figures). http://cta.ornl.gov.

Department of Environment, Food and Rural Affairs. *Action Plan to Develop Organic Food and Farming in England* (DEFRA). London, 2002.

Energy Information Administration. *Annual Energy Review 2005* (on data for figure 5).

ENO Transportation Foundation and National Transportation Statistics (on motorized transportation in the United States).

Garnett, T. *Wise Moves: Exploring the Relationship Between Food, Transport and CO2.* Transport 2000 Trust, 2003.

Goldman Sachs Economic Research (on future transport contribution to carbon emissions).

Hobbs F., and N. Stoops. *Census 2000 Special reports: Demographic trends in the 20th century.* Washington DC, U.S. Government Printing Office, 2002.

International Civil Aviation Organisation (on global air traffic).

International Energy Agency. *Global CO2 Emissions from Fuel Combustion, 2004* (per capita figures).

Jones, A. *Eating Oil — Food Supply in a Changing Climate.* Sustain, London, and

Elm Farm Research Centre, Newbury, 2001 (on the issue of food miles and fuel use).

Keppler, F., J. T. G. Hamilton, M. Brass, and T. Röckmann. "Methane Emissions from Terrestrial Plants under Aerobic Conditions." *Nature* 439, 2006.

King, David, UK chief scientific adviser (statement on the prospects for nuclear fusion), 16 December 2005.

Lawrence, F. and S. Millar, eds. "Food: The Way We Eat Now." *Guardian,* 10 May 2003.

Leggett, J. *Half Gone: Oil, Gas, Hot Air, and the Coming Global Energy Crisis.* London: Portobello Books, 2006.

Leopold Center for Agriculture (on 2001 study of changes in food miles in United States).

Lynas, M. *High Tide: The Truth About Our Climate Crisis.* England: HarperCollins, 2005.

McNeill, J. *Something New Under the Sun: An Environmental History of the Twentieth Century.* London: Penguin Books, 2000.

Meier, A. Lawrence Berkeley National Laboratory Report, 2002 (on electricity leaking in homes).

National Household Travel Survey, 2001 (on extent of walking and bicycling).

National Transport Research Center, Oak Ridge National Laboratory, U.S. Department of Energy (special tabulations on changes in U.S. patterns of shopping, private communication dated 19 January 2006).

Open University. *Working with Our Environment: Technology for a Sustainable Future, Theme 3, Food Chains,* T172. Open University, Milton Keynes, 2001.

ORNL Transportation *Energy Data Book* 24 (on car density in the United States).

PIU. "Energy Scenarios to 2020." 2001. www.piu.gov.uk/2002/energy/workingpapers.shtml.

Rajan, S. C. *Climate Change Dilemma: Technology, Social Change or Both? An Examination of Long-term Transport Policy Choices in the United States.* Energy Policy, 2004 (on contribution of aviation to United States' greenhouse gas emissions).

Renewable Energy Consumption Survey (RECS).

Smil, V. *Energy at the Crossroads.* Cambridge, Mass: MIT Press, 2003.

Sustainable Development Commission Web site: www.sd-commission.gov.uk/.

United Nations. *World Population Prospects: the 2000 Revision and World Urbanization Prospects: The 2001 Revision.* Population

Division of the Department of Economic and Social Affairs of the UN Secretariat, 2002. www.esa.un.org/unpp.

Travel Industry Association of America (for data on U.S. travel).

U.S. Bureau of National Statistics (on energy use, carbon emissions, and freight transport).

U.S. Census Bureau, 2005 (on population figures).

U.S. Department of Energy (on data from survey on residential energy consumption). www.eia.doe.gov/emeu/consumption.

World Business Council for Sustainable Development. *Pathways to 2050 — Energy and Climate Change,* 2005.

World Energy Council. "Global Energy Scenarios to 2050 and Beyond," 2003. www.worldenergy.org/wec-geis/edc/scenario.asp.

Worldwatch Institute. *Vital Signs 2005–2006* (on carbon emissions from U.S. motor gasoline use and on air travel growth).

WWF Living Planet Report, 2004.

3. EYES WIDE SHUT

ABC News, polls in June and October 2005 (on attitudes to climate change).

Brewer, Thomas L. *US Public Opinion on*

Climate Change Issues. Brussels: Centre for European Policy Studies, January 2006 (based on Program on International Political Attitudes [PIPA] and Oak Ridge Center for Advanced Studies [ORCAS] polls conducted in 2005).

Buncombe, Andrew. "Bush Tried to Gag Environment Expert." *The Independent,* 30 January 2006. http://news .independent.co.uk/environment/article 341945.ece.

Cohen, S. *States of Denial: Knowing About Atrocities and Suffering.* London: Polity Press, 2000.

Zogby International Poll in 2005 (on the voluntary approach to reducing greenhouse gases).

4. WISHFUL THINKING

Alliance to Save Energy 2005. Building on success: policies to reduce energy waste in buildings.

American Solar Energy Society. *Proceedings of the ASES 2003 Annual Meeting.*

American Wind Energy Association. *Wind Power Outlook,* 2004 (on area needed for wind turbines). www.awea.org/pubs/ documents/outlook2004.pdf.

Arvizu, Dan, director of National Renewable Energy Laboratory (on projected global energy consumption).

Bailie, A., et al. *Hydrogen Transitions in a Greenhouse Gas Constrained World.* Boston: Tellus Institute, in press (on future prospects for carbon sequestration, hydrogen for transportation, energy efficiency programs, and use of renewables).

Blair, Tony, UK prime minister, in speech at a Conference of the Clinton Global Initiative. New York: 15 September 2005.

Broadmeadow, Mark, and Robert Matthews. "Forests, Carbon and Climate Change: the UK Contribution." Information Note, Forestry Commission, June 2003 (on absorption of carbon dioxide by trees), Edinburgh, Scotland: Forestry Commission. www.forestry.gov.uk.

Brown, M. A., F. Southworth, and T. K. Stovell. *Towards a Climate-Friendly Built Environment,* 2005. Pew Center on Global Climate Change (on energy savings in buildings).

Bush, George W., U.S. president's statements on 11 June 2001, 14 February 2002, and 30 June 2005 (on the role of technology).

Eyre, M., N. Fergusson, and R. Mills. *Fuelling Road Transport.* National Society for Clean Air, Energy Saving Trust and Institute for European Environment Policy, 2002.

Factor 10 Institute: www.factor10-institute.org.

Fawcett, T., A. Hurst, and B. Boardman. *Carbon UK.* University of Oxford: Environmental Change Institute, 2002

——, K. Lane, and B. Boardman. *Lower Carbon Futures.* ECI Research Report 23. University of Oxford: Environmental Change Institute, 2000.

Foley, J. *Tomorrow's Low Carbon Cars: Driving Innovation and Long Term Investment in Low Carbon Cars.* London: IPPR, 2003 (on emissions from LPG vehicles).

Gough, C., S. Shackley, and M. Cannell. "Evaluating the Options for Carbon Sequestration." Tyndall Centre for Climate Change Research, Technical Report 2, 2002. www.tyndall.ac.uk/research/theme2/final_reports/it1_22.pdf.

Global Wind Energy Council: www.gwec.net/.

Guardian. "Row Erupts over Sellafield Security," 7 March 2002 (on consequences of airplane strike on a nuclear power station). www.guardian.co.uk.

International Atomic Energy Agency (on the costs of cleaning up nuclear waste). www.sd-commission.gov.uk/pubs/rp/

index.htm.

Milne, G., and B. Boardman. *Making Cold Homes Warmer: The Effect of Energy Efficiency Improvements in Low Income Homes.* EAGA Partnership Charitable Trust, 1997.

MTC, U.S. Department of Energy, and GE Release Framework for Finding (report on U.S. wind energy potential). www.mtpc.org/renewableenergy/press/pr_9_30_05_wind.htm.

National Bureau of Economic Research, Massachusetts (report on economic growth and sustainable development), 2003.

National Renewable Energy Laboratory (report on the efficiencies of future PV systems).

Renewable Energy World (on costs of photovoltaic systems), September/October 2005 (on the costs of decommissioning nuclear plants and on biodiesel generation, November/December 2005).

Richmond, R., D. Jones, S. Still, J. Curry, and C. Bircher. *Utility Success Stories in Solar Water Heating.* Austin, Texas: National Solar Energy Conference, June 2003.

Royal Society. *The Role of Land Carbon Sinks in Mitigating Global Climate Change.*

London: Royal Society, 2001. www.royal
soc.ac.uk.

Royal Society and Royal Academy of Engineering. *Nuclear Energy: The Future Climate.* London: Royal Society, 1999.

Soil Use and Management. www.ingenta
connect.com/content/cabi/sum.

Sustainable Development Commission.
*Achieving a Better Quality of Life: Annual
Report 2003.* London: Stationery Office,
2003.

——. *Redefining Prosperity: Resource Pro-
ductivity, Economic Growth, and Sustainable Development* (SDC report), 2003.
www.sd-commission.org.uk/
publications.php?id=41.

United States Mission to the European
Union, quoting President Bush's position
on the role of technology, 17 December
2004 and 5 July 2005.

U.S. Department of Energy. *Comprehensive
Analysis of Clean Energy Futures in 2000.*
http://www.ornl.gov/sci/eere/cef.

U.S. Department of Energy, Energy Efficiency and Energy Renewables (on geothermal energy). http://www.eere.energy
.gov/RE/geo_basics.html.

U.S. Department of Energy, Hydrogen
Program and National Renewable Energy
Laboratory.

U.S. Energy Information Administration (on development of "biodiesel" fuel and on forecast increase in energy use by 2025).

von Weizsacker, E. U., A. Lovins, and H. Lovins. *Factor Four: Doubling Wealth, Halving Resource Use.* London: Earthscan, 1997.

Worldwatch Institute. *Vital Signs 2005–2006* (on new nuclear capacity, hybrids in the U.S. automobile market, and use of solar energy).

5. FIDDLING WHILE ROME BURNS

American Council for an Energy Efficient Economy, Washington, DC (on CHP capacity). http://www.aceee.org/energy/chp.htm.

American Wind Energy Association. *Wind Power Outlook,* 2004 (U.S. states with wind turbines).

Blue Green Alliance (on reconciling an expanding economy with environmental protection). www.bluegreenalliance.com/index_original.htm.

Brown, M. A., F. Southworth, and T. K. Stovell. *Towards a Climate-Friendly Built Environment,* 2005. Pew Center on Global Climate Change (on energy savings in buildings).

DeLucchi, Mark. "The Annualized Social Cost of Motor-Vehicle Use in the U.S., 1990–1991: Summary of Theory, Data, Methods, and Results." University of California, Davis (on transportation users paying for only part of damage from climate change). http://www.itc.uc davis.edu.

Environmental Protection Agency. *Environmental Impacts of Removing National Speed Limit Requirements.* Memorandum from Bob Noland to Regional Air Chiefs, 30 November 1995. http://www.epa.gov/otaq/invntory/envspmem.txt.

Hillman, M. "The Future of Public Transport: The Dangers of Viewing Policy Through Rose-tinted Spectacles." In Whitelegg J., and G. Haq, eds. *The Earthscan Reader on World Transport Policy & Practice.* London: Earthscan, 2003.

International Energy Agency. *Oil Crises and Climate Challenges: 30 Years of Energy Use in IEA Countries.* Paris, France: International Energy Agency, 2004 (on energy-intensity improvement and on oil reserves and consumption).

Kennedy, R. F. *Crimes Against Nature.* New York: HarperCollins, 2004.

Komanoff, Charles. "Transportation Elasticities: How Prices Affect Travel Behavior." Victoria Transport Policy Institute, 2005 (on effect of fuel price on reducing driving). www.vtpi.org/gasoline_elasticity .xls.

Pucher, John, and John Renne. "Socioeconomics of Urban Travel: Evidence from the 2001 NHTS." *Transportation Quarterly* 57, no. 3, 2003 (on decreases in public transportation use). http:// policy.rutgers.edu/papers/14.pdf.

U.S. Department of Transportation, Federal Highway Administration. *Highway Statistics 2003.* Washington, DC.

White House *Fact Sheet* on President Bush's position on climate change, 18 May 2005.

6. TURNING THE TANKER AROUND

National Academy of Sciences, Division of Earth Sciences, Committee on Climatology (T. F. Malone, chair), 1957. *First General Report on Climatology to the Chief of the Weather Bureau.* Washington, DC: National Academy of Sciences (attempting to balance the costs of mitigation today against future avoided costs of environmental damage from climate change).

Nordhaus, William. Editorial comment,

"Discounting in Economics and Climate Change." *Climate Change* 37, 1997.

7. THE BLUEPRINT FOR SURVIVAL

All Party Parliamentary Group on Climate Change (UK MPs supporting Contraction and Convergence). www.colinchallen .org.uk.

Bodansky, Dan. "International Climate Efforts Beyond 2012: A Survey of Approaches." Pew Center on Global Climate Change, Washington, DC, 2004.

Global Commons Institute: www.gci.org.uk/ links/detail.pdf. See also Royal Commission on Environmental Pollution: www .rcep.org.uk/pdf/chp4.pdf.

Global Commons Network: www.topica .com/lists/GCN@igc.topica.com/read.

Heinrich-Böll-Foundation and the European Climate Forum. A set of dialogues on post-Kyoto proposals: www.kyotoplus .org. See also the German Scientific Advisory Council on Global Environmental Change (WBGU). *Climate Protection Strategies for the 21st Century: Kyoto and Beyond:* www.wbgu_sn2003_presse_engl .html.

Houghton, Sir John, on carbon dioxide concentrations in the atmosphere.

Kartha, S., T. Athanasiou, P. Baer, and D. Cornland. "Cutting the Knot: Climate Protection, Political Realism and Equity as Requirements of a post-Kyoto regime." Report of EcoEquity and Tellus Institute, 15 April 2005. www.ecoequity.org/docs/CuttingTheKnot.pdf.

King, Sir David. UK Government Scientific Adviser, interview in the *Guardian,* 16 December 2005, on future carbon dioxide concentrations in the atmosphere.

Meyer, A. *Contraction and Convergence: The Global Solution to Climate Change.* Totnes: Green Books, 2000.

Nakicenovic, N., and R. Swart. *Emissions Scenarios: Special Report of the Intergovernmental Panel on Climate Change.* Cambridge University Press, 2000.

National Academy of Sciences, Division of Earth Sciences, Committee on Climatology (T. F. Malone, chair), 1957. *First General Report on Climatology to the Chief of the Weather Bureau.* Washington, DC: National Academy of Sciences.

Rosa, L. P., M. S. Muylaert, and C. P. de Campos. *The Brazilian Proposal and its Scientific and Methodological Aspects.* International Virtual Institute on Global Exchange, 1997.

8. Fair Shares for All

Burnett, J. *Plenty and Want: A Social History of Food in England from 1815 to the Present Day,* 3rd edition. London: Routledge, 1989.

Carley, M., I. Christie, and M. Hillman. "Towards the Next Environment White Paper." *Policy Studies* 12, no. 1, 1991 (on the proposal for carbon rationing).

Hillman, M. "Why Climate Change Must Top the Agenda" and "Carbon Budget Watchers." In Hillman, M. ed., "Special Section: Climate change." *Town and Country Planning,* October 1998.

Intergovernmental Panel on Climate Change. *Special Report on Aviation and the Upper Atmosphere,* eds. J. E. Penner, D. H. Lister, D. J. Griggs, D. J. Dokken, and M. McFarland. England: Cambridge University Press, 1999.

National Energy Foundation. *Simple Ways to Save Energy.* National Energy Foundation, 2003.

Royal Commission on Environmental Pollution. *Energy: The Changing Climate,* twenty-second report, 2000, and *The Environmental Effects of Civil Aircraft in Flight.* London: Stationery Office, 2002.

Starkey, R., and A. Anderson. *Domestic*

Tradable Quotas: A Policy Instrument for Reducing Greenhouse Gas Emissions from Energy Use. Technical Report 39. Tyndall Centre for Climate Change Research, 2005. http://www.tyndall.ac.uk/research/theme2/final_reports/t3_22.pdf.

UK Government Sustainable Development: www.sustainable-development.gov.uk.

World Commission on Environment and Development. *Our Common Future* (the Brundtland Report). England: Oxford University Press, 1987.

Zweiniger-Bargielowska, I. *Austerity in Britain: Rationing, Controls and Consumption, 1939–1955.* England: Oxford University Press, 2000.

9. Carbon Watchers

Agras, J., and D. Chapman. "The Kyoto Protocol, CAFE Standards, and Gasoline Taxes." *Contemporary Economic Policy,* March 1999.

Boardman, B., T. Fawcett, H. Griffin, M. Hinnells, K. Lane, and J. Palmer. *2MtC: Two Million Tonnes of Carbon.* University of Oxford: Environmental Change Institute, 1997.

Center for Sustainable Energy Systems, Personal Transportation Fact Sheets,

University of Michigan (on personal travel data in the United States). http://css.snre.umich.edu/css_doc/CSS01-07.pdf.

Environmental Protection Agency. www.epa.gov/epahome; http://yosemite.epa.gov/oar/globalwarming.nsf/content/ResourceCenterPublicationsGHGEmissionsUSEmissionsInventory2006.html.

Greene, D. L., and S. E. Plotkin. "Energy Futures for the US Transport Sector." *Energy Policy* 29, issue 14, November 2001.

Hillman, M. "In favour of the Compact City." In Jenks, M., E. Burton, and K. Williams, eds., *The Compact City: A Sustainable Urban Form?* London: E.&F.N.Spon, 1996.

———. "The Future of Air Travel and International Tourism." *World Transport Policy and practice.*3, no.1, 1997.

———. "The Relevance of Climate Change to Future Policy on Walking and Cycling." In Tolley, R., ed., *Sustainable Transport.* Abington, England: Woodhead Publishing, 2003.

Jardine, C. *Calculating the Environmental Impacts of Aviation Emissions.* University of Oxford: Environmental Change Institute, 2005.

Palmer, J., and B. Boardman. *DELight: Domestic Efficient Lighting.* University of Oxford: Environmental Change Institute, 1998.

References for table 2: Environmental Protection Agency, http://yosemite .epa.gov/oar/globalwarming.nsf/content/ ResourceCenterPublicationsGHG EmissionsUSEmissionsInventory2006 .html; Penner, J. E., D. H. Lister, D. J. Griggs, D. J. Dokken, and M. McFarland. "Aviation and the Global Atmosphere." A Special Report of the Intergovernmental Panel on Climate Change. England: Cambridge University Press, 2000.

Royal Commission on Environmental Pollution, *The Environmental Effects of Aircraft in Flight,* SS2002.

U.S. Department of Transportation, Federal Highway Administration, reports. www .fhwa.dot.gov/ohim/bluebook.pdf.

10. CONCLUSIONS

Ekins, P., M. Hillman, and R. Hutchison. *Wealth Beyond Measure.* London: Gaia Books, 1992.

Hillman, M. "Ethical Implications of Climate Change for Personal Lifestyles." *Ethical Record,* September 2001.

Houghton, J. "Global warming is now a weapon of mass destruction." *Guardian,* 28 July 2003.

Lovelock, James. *The Revenge of Gaia.* London: Allen Lane, 2006.

BIOGRAPHIES

Mayer Hillman qualified as an architect and town planner at University College London in the mid-1950s and for thirteen years was a partner in private practice. He then worked on his doctoral thesis at the University of Edinburgh on the links between transportation, planning, and environmental issues. In 1970, he joined the Policy Studies Institute (formerly called Political and Economic Planning) as the head of its Environment and Quality of Life Research Program until 1992. He is now senior fellow emeritus at the institute. His focus has been on transportation, urban planning, energy conservation, health promotion, road safety, and environment policies. He is the author or coauthor of numerous publications on these subjects. For nearly forty years, his research has shown that public policy should be more socially and environmentally conscious and pay far more attention to issues of equity. He was one of the first proponents of personal carbon rationing as the only realistic way for the world's population to prevent serious damage from climate change.

Tina Fawcett is a senior researcher at the Environmental Change Institute, University of Oxford. She specializes in personal energy use and climate change and has been working in this field for the past decade. Recently she completed her doctorate at University College London on household energy use, carbon emissions, and personal carbon allowances. She is author and co-author of several publications on household energy use and carbon dioxide emissions.

Sudhir Chella Rajan is a senior fellow at the Tellus Institute in Boston, where he leads the Global Politics and Institutions Program. He has an extensive background in transportation energy systems, and the institutional and political context of environmental policy making. He is broadly concerned with the interactions among social, political, technological, and environmental factors relating to sustainable development. He is the author of *The Enigma of Automobility: Democratic Politics and Pollu-*

tion Control (University of Pittsburgh Press). He has a doctoral degree in Environmental Science and Engineering from the University of California, Los Angeles.

The employees of Thorndike Press hope you have enjoyed this Large Print book. All our Thorndike and Wheeler Large Print titles are designed for easy reading, and all our books are made to last. Other Thorndike Press Large Print books are available at your library, through selected bookstores, or directly from us.

For information about titles, please call:
  (800) 223-1244

or visit our Web site at:
  www.gale.com/thorndike
  www.gale.com/wheeler

To share your comments, please write:
  Publisher
  Thorndike Press
  295 Kennedy Memorial Drive
  Waterville, ME 04901